Restless
Faith

Restless Faith

Holding Evangelical Beliefs
in a World of Contested Labels

Richard J. Mouw

BrazosPress

a division of Baker Publishing Group
Grand Rapids, Michigan

Published by Brazos Press
a division of Baker Publishing Group
PO Box 6287, Grand Rapids, MI 49516-6287
www.brazospress.com

Printed in the United States of America

Library of Congress Cataloging-in-Publication Data
Names: Mouw, Richard J., author.
Title: Restless faith : holding evangelical beliefs in a world of contested labels / Richard J. Mouw.
Description: Grand Rapids, MI : Brazos Press, [2019] | Includes bibliographical references and index.
Identifiers: LCCN 2018028041 | ISBN 9781587433924 (pbk. : alk. paper)
Subjects: LCSH: Evangelicalism—United States. | Christianity and culture—United States.
Classification: LCC BR1642.U5 M68 2019 | DDC 277.3/082—dc23
LC record available at https://lccn.loc.gov/2018028041

ISBN 978-1-58743-433-4 (casebound)

19 20 21 22 23 24 25   7 6 5 4 3 2 1

Contents

Acknowledgments

At several points I draw from short articles and bits and pieces from longer essays that I have published over the last decade; these are acknowledged in footnotes. I also make use of ideas presented in my 2013–14 Parchman Lectures at Baylor University's Truett Theological Seminary at several points. In chapters 13 and 14 I touch on matters that I explored in more detail in my 2015–16 Kent Mathews Lectures at Denver Seminary.

1

The Label Question

When I was thinking about an appropriate title for this book, I was tempted to take my cue from the late singer Prince, who in 1993 decided he no longer wanted to be called Prince. Indeed, he said, he no longer wanted to be known by any name at all. The folks who arranged his concerts did not like that idea, and after trying out several names—with suggestions from Prince's fans—the singer agreed to this one: The Artist Formerly Known as Prince.

All of this came to mind as I was contemplating different word choices to sum up what this book is about. From the beginnings of my adult career as a teacher-scholar I have identified closely with American evangelicalism. Not that I have always been comfortable with everything associated with that label, but my discomfort has never been strong enough to make me want to move to other spiritual-theological environs. My original plan for this book was to highlight both the discomfort and the commitment by using the phrase "restless evangelical" in the title.

During the time that I have been writing this book, however, there has been considerable debate about whether "evangelical" is still a useful label. I won't go into the details that have given rise to this debate, except to say that for a variety of reasons "evangelical" has come to be seen by many as referring to a highly politicized form of Christianity here in North America.

I don't think the debate is a silly one. My own discomfort with identifying as an evangelical has certainly increased in the past few years. And some folks whom I have known and admired in the evangelical movement have said publicly that they can no longer own the label. I have taken their concerns seriously—which is why I thought of this Prince-inspired title: The Movement Formerly Known as Evangelicalism.

I think it will be clear to the readers of this book why I am not ready, though, to join the "formerly known as" movement. I still think the label stands for something wonderfully important, and I am not ready to give the label over to those who advocate an angry Religious Right politics. I will explain at a couple of points in these pages why I personally still hold on to the label.

But—and this is important for me to emphasize at the beginning—I do not want the legitimacy of what I will be discussing in these pages to depend on the continued viability of the label. Suppose that ten years from now "evangelical" no longer means what it has in the past, as applied to a distinct movement within global Christianity. I hope the distinctives that the label once stood for will still be widely accepted. While I will be discussing here the reasons why I personally continue to find "evangelical" a viable descriptor, then, what I really care about is that the folks who are gravitating toward a "formerly known as" identity will still hold on to what has been the distinct spiritual and theological *legacy* of evangelicalism.

Like so many of my friends, I have no desire to be associated with the politicized excesses of present-day evangelicalism. But there is much in what many of us have loved in the evangelicalism of the past that we—under whatever label we choose to describe ourselves from here on—should not abandon.

I don't want to come off as defensive about my own preference for holding on to the label. I think it is a healthy thing to argue about whether a label like "evangelical" has outlived its usefulness. Indeed, for most of my life as an evangelical I have been engaged in conversations—some of them extended arguments—about what it means to be an evangelical. Those have been important exercises for me. So, while not wanting to turn this book into an extended defense for keeping the label, I do want to explain at the outset some of my reasons for hoping that we do not abandon that way of describing ourselves. Then I will add some more reasons, briefly, at the end of this book.

| Holding On to the Label

The Institute for the Study of American Evangelicals was established at Wheaton College in 1982, and it ended its existence in 2014. But while it lasted it was a wonderful gathering place for evangelical scholarly discussion. The historians Mark Noll and Nathan Hatch were the founders, and they had a knack for bringing interesting people together to explore fascinating topics. In the early years we often argued quite a bit about the "evangelical" label itself. Someone would come up with a proposal about what makes for being an evangelical, and someone else would respond that there were a lot of Catholics who fit the description. So we would go back to the drawing board.

In 1989 a British evangelical historian, David Bebbington, published a book in which he proposed a four-part definition of "evangelical," and his account pretty much put an end to the debates. His proposal, which has come to be known as "the Beb-bington quadrilateral," identified these four distinctively evan-gelical emphases: (1) we believe in the *need for conversion*—making a personal commitment to Christ as Savior and Lord; (2) we hold to the *Bible's supreme authority*—the *sola scriptura* theme of the Reformation; (3) we emphasize a *cross-centered theology*—at the heart of the gospel is the atoning work of Jesus on the cross of Calvary; and (4) we insist on an *active faith*—not just Sunday worship, but daily discipleship.[1]

Of course, plenty of Christians who do not self-identify as evangelicals can claim each of those features. And some can even hold all four of them together. What strikes me as distinc-tively evangelical about the four features of the quadrilateral is, first of all, that these items are *singled out* as key theological basics, and second, that they are *held* in a certain way.

On the singling-out point: I have Protestant friends who would certainly endorse all four points while not claiming the "evangelical" label in the way we were trying to account for it in our Wheaton debates. The response of these Protestant folks would be: "Yes, sure—but why just those four?" Some Anglicans would be reluctant to affirm biblical authority with-out quickly adding something about the role of tradition. My Lutheran friends would not balk at a central emphasis on con-version and the cross but would see those as lacking enough specific content if "justification by faith alone" were not added as one of the essentials for understanding the others. And some of these same folks would also want to pay attention to eccle-siological specifics and the central role of the Eucharist.

As an evangelical, I don't think it is wrongheaded to pay close attention to such things. But the items in the quadrilateral

1. David W. Bebbington, *Evangelicalism in Modern Britain: A History from the 1730s to the 1980s* (London: Unwin Hyman, 1989), 2–17.

are for me theological emphases that serve to unite a trans-denominational, transconfessional movement. I may wish that a Baptist evangelical had a more robust appreciation for the sealing of God's covenant promises in the baptism of infants. But that area of disagreement is not as basic as the matters set forth in Bebbington's quadrilateral.

A case in point: I have rather strong affinities for a fairly detailed ecclesiology, and I am willing to argue at length with folks who disagree with me on these matters. But I am also very fond of the sentiment that Alister McGrath, himself an Anglican evangelical, expresses in response to the complaint that we evangelicals are willing to tolerate weak ecclesiologies. Yes, he observes, we evangelicals do often operate with an "underdeveloped ecclesiology"—but we are willing to live with that defect because of what we have experienced at the hands of "others who have over-developed ecclesiologies."[2]

And that, of course, points to the factor of how we evangelicals *hold to* what we see as the basics. It is impossible to understand why the four points of the quadrilateral loom so large for us without understanding our own histories.

The question about how evangelicals hold to the basics came up in the question-and-answer period after a lecture I gave on a Catholic campus. This university had a significant number of evangelical students, and they invited me to speak about the relationship between Catholics and evangelicals. I had explained the Bebbington quadrilateral in my lecture, and a student in the audience responded in a rather blunt fashion: "My response as a Catholic to those four points you mentioned is 'Duh!' What's so special about those points? As a Catholic I can endorse them too!"

2. Alister McGrath, "Evangelical Anglicanism: A Contradiction in Terms?," in *Evangelical Anglicans: Their Role and Influence in the Church Today*, ed. R. T. France and A. E. McGrath (London: SPCK, 1993), 14.

Afterward my host, a Catholic priest theologian, put the point in more detail. "I can agree with all four of your Bebbington points," he said. "Certainly three of them are for me no-brainers. Do we need to have a personal relationship to Christ? Of course. Is the cross essential for atonement? Yes, surely. An activist faith? Why would we deny that? But even the supremacy of the Bible works for us in an important sense. Biblical revelation has primacy for us—it's just that we insist on an infallible church authority in deciding how to *interpret* the Bible!"

I could have pushed him on several specifics in what he was saying, but his overall observation was legitimate. For evangelicals the four emphases of the Bebbington quadrilateral are just that: *emphases*. And they are emphases that have a lot of history attached to them. They are lines that in the past we have drawn in the sand in the midst of specific controversies.

We have insisted on the need for a personal relationship to Christ in response to a more "nominal" form of Christianity—as well as over against a "many different roads to heaven" relativism. We have proclaimed the supremacy of the Bible's authority as over against those who allow churchly authority to "correct," or to supplement in relativizing ways, the clear teachings of the Scriptures. The centrality of the work of the cross has been for us a nonnegotiable undergirding of the call to sinners to trust in Christ alone as the heaven-sent Savior. And our brand of activism has been our way of insisting that a genuine faith must take shape in the kind of holy living that requires us to bear witness to God's revealed will for our daily lives.

All of that still strikes me as of great importance. And the word "evangelical"—from "evangel," the gospel—has been for me a perfectly fine shorthand label for covering that theological and spiritual territory.

| Still Viable?

Again, though, as I write this, many people who have identified as evangelical in the past are wondering whether it is time to give up on "evangelical" as a term of self-identification.

Sometimes the concern is raised by people who think that preserving labels as such is a bad practice. When an op-ed piece that I wrote, defending the continuing use of the label, appeared online, someone posted a comment characterizing my defense as "tribalism." Well, in a certain sense, yes. I prefer to characterize evangelicalism as a movement, but we are also a tribe of sorts. And there are also other tribes, with whom we have long-standing differences. It doesn't help, then, simply to stick with being "Christian"—also a tribal label, of course. There is enough serious diversity in Christianity to require some further specificity regarding where one places oneself on the broad Christian spectrum. I find the need for a label that distinguishes my pattern of Christian from many others.

There is also a very practical issue about abandoning the "evangelical" label. The Fellowship of Evangelical Seminary Presidents, for example, meets for a few days each January in a retreat setting. It is in its own way a diverse group: conservative Reformed types, Holiness, Pentecostal, Baptist, Anabaptist, "none of the above"—all quite willing, and even eager, to gather together under the "evangelical" label.

Suppose they decide that because of the recent connections of the label to right-wing politics they should change the name of their organization to "The Fellowship of _____ Seminary Presidents": How would they fill in the blank? If they chose "Christian" they would have to make it clear that not just any president of any seminary who claimed that identification would be comfortable in their midst. "Historically Christian"?

Once again, the label would require some explaining. Or "Orthodox"? The very fact that they would have to use a capital letter would compel them to explain that they were not claiming to have converted to *that* kind of Orthodoxy.

For myself, I can't think of a label that suits me better than "evangelical." For one thing, it affirms my ties to people in the past who felt strongly about using it to define their understanding of their Christian identity: Sunday school teachers, youth ministers, family members, missionaries—and many of my own saints and heroes: Billy Graham, Carl Henry, Leighton Ford, Elizabeth Eliott, Tom Skinner, Corrie Ten Boom, Vernon Grounds, Arthur Holmes, Edward Carnell, Dave Hubbard, to name only a few.

One of the vows that the Benedictine monks take is the vow of stability. To take that vow is to pledge to stick with a particular monastic community. Many of us in the older generation of evangelicals have taken something like that vow in our relationship to our movement. There is much to consider in deciding whether to break that vow.

| A New Generation

One consideration in deciding whether evangelical identity is worth preserving is our relationship to our younger generation. Take Amy—not her real name—a Fuller Seminary student. She was raised by evangelical parents who were active in a conservative congregation. Amy's own faith was strengthened by her participation during high school in Young Life. She attended an evangelical college, where she embraced the idea of developing Christian worldview sensitivities—including a strong commitment to marginalized peoples. Amy is now in seminary, studying cross-cultural ministries. She wants to bring the healing power of the gospel to women who have been deeply wounded by sex trafficking.

Amy loves her parents, but she has a difficult time these days talking with them about the things that matter most to her. Her mom and dad are numbered among the 81 percent of "white evangelicals" who voted for Donald Trump in the 2016 presidential election. Her parents suspect that Barack Obama is secretly a Muslim, and they also wish that many Latinos living in the United States could be "sent back to where they came from."

Amy loves Jesus, and she believes that the Bible is God's supremely authoritative Word. She leans toward the traditional understanding of marriage, but she stays in touch with friends she knew well in Young Life who have subsequently come out as openly gay and lesbian.

Right now Amy isn't sure whether she wants to be known as an evangelical: "The label has gotten too politicized." The practical challenge for her is where she goes denominationally.

I met Amy's mother once, when she visited our campus. She was clearly proud of Amy, and the affection between them was obvious. I wish she and Amy could find more common ground on the issues where they presently disagree. I'm sure that Amy's parents are troubled by some of her views, but they do not see her as having simply departed from the faith of her younger days.

Both Amy and her parents are a part of my evangelical world. I want to see Amy's parents move in Amy's direction on many of their social and political views. I want Amy to claim the evangelical faith of her upbringing. As an evangelical educator I sense an obligation to both Amy and her parents. If I have to take sides, though, I will cast my lot with Amy, encouraging her also to take a vow of stability. I don't want the evangelical movement to lose her. We need her.

| The Elites[3]

The *New York Times* columnist Ross Douthat has written about what he sees as a possible "crackup" that may be coming in the evangelical community.[4] He sees a quiet version of that split already happening within the younger generation—Amy and her peers—some of whom seem to be quietly moving in other directions: mainline Protestantism, Catholicism, Orthodoxy.

The more dramatic gap, as Douthat sees it, is between the elites—"evangelical intellectuals and writers, and their friends in other Christian traditions"—and those millions of folks who worship in evangelical churches. It may be, he says, that these elites "have overestimated how much a serious theology has ever mattered to evangelicalism's sociological success." It could be that the views and attitudes on display in the recent support for rightist causes has really been there all along, without much of an interest in the kinds of intellectual-theological matters that have preoccupied the elites. If so, then the elites will eventually go off on their own, leaving behind an evangelicalism that is "less intellectual, more partisan, more racially segregated"—a movement that is in reality "not all that greatly changed" from what it has actually been in the past.[5]

Douthat hopes he is wrong about this, and I think he is. But his scenario gets some plausibility from the evangelical elites who have been talking about leaving "evangelical" behind.

3. Parts of this section have been adapted from Richard J. Mouw, "The Unlikely Crackup of Evangelicalism," *Christianity Today*, January 3, 2018, https://www.christianitytoday.com/ct/2018/january-web-only/unlikely-crack-up-of-evangelicalism.html. Used with permission.

4. Ross Douthat, "Is There an Evangelical Crisis?," editorial, *New York Times*, November 25, 2017, https://www.nytimes.com/2017/11/25/opinion/sunday/trump-evangelical-crisis.html.

5. Douthat, "Is There an Evangelical Crisis?"

This scenario does not really hold up well, though, when we look at the realities of evangelicalism's intellectual community. Douthat's picture is one of a band of "evangelical intellectuals" who are cut off from much of the vast majority of "ordinary" evangelicals. Is that picture accurate?

There is a rather significant network of evangelical academic institutions in North America. The Council of Christian Colleges and Universities (CCCU) has a membership of 140 evangelical schools, with a total enrollment of over 300,000 students. In addition, the Association of Theological Schools (ATS) reports that of the 270 member institutions that it accredits in North America, 40 percent of these seminaries identify themselves as evangelical, and their student bodies account for 60 percent—about 40,000 students—of those enrolled in graduate theological education. If we add to those numbers the many Bible institutes, colleges, and seminaries who are not members of either the CCCU or the ATS, it is fair to say that "evangelical intellectuals" are presently teaching almost half a million students who have chosen to attend self-identified evangelical schools.

The majority of those students come from evangelical churches, and many will return to those churches. They will also take what they have learned from "evangelical intellectuals" into professional life when they graduate. This is not exactly a picture of ivory tower elites who are clueless about grassroots evangelicalism.

As one who has spent over a half century in the evangelical academy, I have just sketched a picture that poses some important questions for my own reflection. Given the tens of thousands of evangelical students whom my colleagues and I have taught, to what degree are we responsible for current attitudes and viewpoints in the evangelical movement at large? And if we were to decide to "resign" from evangelicalism, would we have an obligation to all of those former students, to give them counsel about what they should now do with what we have taught them about being "evangelical"?

I also have a different sort of concern, relating to what I described earlier about those conferences we had in previous decades at the Institute for the Study of American Evangelicalism. When we came together—there and in other venues—to talk about an evangelical identity that we all claimed at the time, we experienced a shared commitment to addressing a diverse intellectual agenda out of a deep commitment to the gospel. This bonding produced, in turn, a kind of scholarship that we would not have otherwise pursued if we had not seen ourselves as serving a distinct movement within American Christianity.

What happens to all of that now? Is that kind of bonding in the evangelical academy no longer needed? Will younger scholars continue to nurture those bonds if they no longer have a sense of serving a broader spiritual-theological movement?

A well-known scholar—himself a secular Jew—once spent some time working on a project at Fuller Seminary. He was a good friend, and he made a point of sharing with me his impressions of what he experienced at Fuller. "This is a unique place, Richard," he said. "Right now your faculty is holding two things together in an impressive manner. You have top-notch scholarship *and* you have strong connections to the grass roots." Then he went on: "But you can't keep that up. Eventually you will either dumb down your scholarship or you will lose touch with the grass roots. Holding the two in tension is great while it lasts, but it will inevitably come apart."

I responded by telling him that Fuller was only one of many evangelical campuses where the successful holding-together was happening. And I said I was confident we could all keep doing it well. Indeed, I said, if the day comes when we go in one or the other directions he described, I would consider it a major defeat for evangelicalism as such.

Douthat's "crackup" scenario is, in effect, a prediction that the defeat is coming. It does not have to happen that way, though. Nor does being successful at the holding-together require necessarily keeping the "evangelical" label. But it does mean intentionally developing a clear strategy for preserving what has been the best of the legacy that has—up to now—been identified by that label. I plead with those intellectual leaders who have been talking about simply resigning from the evangelical movement to stay around and help to work on that strategy.

2

A Faith in Motion

Christianity is on the move these days. The church is growing in the global south—Latin America, Africa, Asia—while decreasing in the Northern Hemisphere. New cultural realities have brought new challenges. As a theologian who tries to pay careful attention to what is happening in our cultural context, I am thinking these days about matters that were not even on my intellectual radar at the beginning of my career: sexual identities, social media, online shopping, gaming, video streaming, alt-right politics, drones, clones, virtual reality.

We may wish that we would not have to pay close attention to all of this, but we ignore these realities at great peril for the church and its mission. For my part, I do find some of this to be exciting to wrestle with. For most of my journey as a Christian, and more specifically as an evangelical, I have been aware of being in motion.

| Standing Fast

The folks who raised me in the faith—parents, teachers, preachers, evangelists—made much of the importance of standing in the faith. We were to stand fast. If there was any encouragement to associate movement with that standing, it was usually a vertical movement: "stand *up* for Jesus," while we are "standing on the promises."

That emphasis on staying in place spiritually was fed in large part by the memories of the fundamentalist versus modernist battles in the earlier decades of the twentieth century. Often in those years the image of being in motion was associated with the liberal rhetoric of "progressing" and "evolving" and looking forward rather than backward theologically. I heard many stories of courageous leaders who had "taken a stand for the gospel" by opposing the rise of liberal theology, and in my teenage years we were encouraged to "stand fast in the faith" in our public high schools.

I am still fine with the standing imagery. I am glad that the younger evangelicals whom I know love to sing "Here in the love of Christ I stand" from Townend and Getty's "In Christ Alone." When Martin Luther declared, "Here I stand, I can do no other," he had good biblical support: "Be on your guard; stand firm in the faith" (1 Cor. 16:13).

Again, there is much that is good and important about the standing imagery. But I have also become attached to the idea of holding on to the faith rather than simply standing on it. The holding image is also biblical: we must "hold firmly to the faith we profess" (Heb. 4:14); Jesus told the early church to "hold on to what you have until I come" (Rev. 2:25).

Here is what I especially like about holding: we can hold on firmly while we are in motion. And I sense that I, like many other evangelicals, have been moving a lot during the past few decades. There are times, to be sure, when we simply have to stop and take a stand. More often than not, however, our lives as Christians these days are about holding fast while we are moving fast.

| From Noun to Gerund

For several decades I have been teaching and writing about the importance of having a Christian worldview. More recently, though, I find myself moving from noun to gerund. None of us can rightly claim simply to "have" a biblically based worldview, in the sense of possessing a fully formed vision of the world and the challenges it presents to us. We can't just enter our questions into a Christian system of thought and expect that system to churn out all the answers. We must engage in world*viewing*, reflecting on what we encounter as the Word illuminates what we see as we journey.

A verse that looms large for me in this regard is Psalm 119:105: "Your word is a lamp for my feet, a light on my path." It feels like we are walking a path these days with many new things suddenly coming into view. A married lesbian couple comes to Christ while visiting an evangelical church, and now they want to join and have their two children baptized. How do we advise them on the next step? What about transgender identities? I haven't really thought seriously about that in the past. Drones as a means of warfare? That raises some new questions for those of us who adhere to Just War theory. Talking to my Muslim neighbors? That has been a new conversation for many of us.

I do not have tried-and-true answers to things of that sort. All I know to do is to seek some kind of clarity of vision as I shine the Word of God on these phenomena as they show up along the pathway.

Does putting the case in that way cause too much confusion, too much uncertainty, for faithful discipleship in today's world? Well, it certainly could. But we can work on developing some helpful resources. Walking the path of faith properly requires exercising *discernment*, which is a spiritual gift that is employed best when it is exercised communally. We need to engage in sustained efforts to train the eyes of faith for seeking the illumination of God's Word on what we see along the way. We read the Word and then we talk together—even arguing with one another—about how we are to respond to the new challenges we are encountering on the path of faith.

"Would You Call This . . . ?"[1]

During my years as a member of the Calvin College Philosophy Department, we held weekly sessions as faculty colleagues to discuss one another's scholarly works-in-progress. At one point Nicholas Wolterstorff was working on a technical book in the philosophy of art, and one week we discussed a chapter on what makes something a work of art.

I asked him a question about something my wife and I had seen recently at an art exhibit in Chicago. One of the artists had created a work by covering a good-sized sheet of plywood with Elmer's Glue. Then he had smashed a cello onto the plywood. When the glue hardened, holding the shattered fragments in place, he exhibited this as a work of art.

"Help me understand that," I said to Wolterstorff. "What is going on there?" His answer stayed with me. Whenever we see a puzzling artwork of this sort, he said, we should think of the artist as at least implicitly asking us this question: "Okay, would you call *this* a work of art?"—thus inviting us to think about the appropriate categories and boundaries for evaluating aesthetic works.

1. Parts of this section are adapted from Richard J. Mouw, "The Problem of Authority in Evangelical Christianity," in *Church Unity and the Papal Office: An Ecumenical Dialogue on John Paul II's Encyclical* Ut Unum Sint, ed. Carl E. Braaten and Robert W. Jensen (Grand Rapids: Eerdmans, 2001), 133–34. Used with permission.

That conversation took place just before "deconstruction" became a much-used term in the academic community. In many Christian minds these days, "deconstruction" stands for some of the worst things that have come to be associated with postmodern thinking. Deconstructionists want us to look at the things we have always taken for granted and pick them apart, subjecting them to a negative critique, even at times holding traditional categories and beliefs up for ridicule. This is certainly what has been happening in our cultural understanding of marriage. "Okay, would you call *this* a marriage?" Why must a marriage be between one man and one woman? Why not a relationship between two persons of the same gender? And—this being asked in several places in Europe these days—why not a relationship among *three* women? Or why do we even have to limit ourselves to labels like "male" and "female"? Why only two categories for deciding a person's gender identity?

Needless to say, I would not be very popular in the evangelical movement if I went around encouraging that spirit of deconstructionism. To focus persistently on traditional understandings of things, making use of what we call these days "a hermeneutic of suspicion," is to open ourselves to an undermining of any sense of a divine ordering of human life.

The fact is, however, that in matters of our congregational life we evangelicals have for several decades now been engaged in our own rather extensive project of deconstruction. We have been—at least implicitly—asking questions of this sort: "Okay, would you call *this* a hymn?" "Would you call *this* a praiseworthy musical instrument?" "Would you call *this* a church building?" "Would you call *this* a congregation?" "Would you call *this* a worship service?" "Would you call *this* a sermon?"

At work here are something like deconstructionist tendencies in evangelicalism's ways of thinking about the life and mission of the church. And this is not a bad thing. Church renewal is good, and in order to be open to the right kind of change we need to keep reexamining our definitions of the forms and patterns of our ministries.

A book that has helped me much in my thinking about the church is *Models of the Church* by the great Jesuit theologian Avery Dulles (appointed a cardinal toward the end of his life). In this book he draws on a study by a biblical scholar from Yale, Paul Minear, who discovered ninety-six images of the church in the New Testament. Dulles sees this as a rich storehouse for our continuing efforts at church renewal. "Under the leading of the Holy Spirit," Dulles writes, "the images and forms of Christian life will continue to change, as they have in previous centuries."[2]

Dulles was no "anything goes" theologian. He was known as one of the more traditionalist thinkers in the post–Vatican II Catholic Church. This makes the sentence I just quoted even more significant. Having pointed us to the Bible as our guide in what we are to think about the church, he says first of all that we need to be open to the "images and forms" of our life together. But he rightly insists, this can happen only by "the leading of the Spirit"—and with an awareness, he quickly adds, of how change has been pursued "in previous centuries."

The Bible, the presence of the Holy Spirit, and an awareness of those who have walked difficult paths in the past—all three are necessary for restless evangelicals to hold fast to the faith.

---

2. Avery Dulles, *Models of the Church: A Critical Assessment of the Church in All Its Aspects* (Garden City, NY: Doubleday, 1974), 192.

| 3 |

A Restless Journey

As I have said already, I am writing this book with my own conviction that it is still a good thing to be evangelical. The word "still" in that sentence carries a lot of baggage right now. To be sure, there have always been people—folks of other religious persuasions and those with no religious persuasion at all—who have not believed that being evangelical is a good thing. And to repeat what I said in introducing all of this, these days some people who have gladly identified themselves with evangelicalism in the past are saying that the movement is not worth the effort to preserve. I disagree. I think that being evangelical is still important. And if others decide to give up the label, I hope we can take special steps together to preserve the legacy.

Since I have spent a half century or so taking evangelical identity seriously, some of what I say here will deal with some personal history. But in writing this I have tried not to make this primarily a book about me. I will talk about my personal journey here—at least, this is my conscious intention—since I find it difficult to make my case without telling some of the stories that have shaped my own continuing efforts to maintain an evangelical identity.

As I write this I am in my midseventies, and I am aware of people my age—especially people who have occupied leadership roles in an organization or movement—getting grumpy about how things are going with the younger generation. We worry that the goals and sensitivities that have guided us and our forebears are not being honored anymore.

That is not my mood as I write this book. My decades of identifying myself as an evangelical have been restless ones, and I still experience that restlessness. When I was installed as Fuller Seminary's president in 1993, I organized my inaugural address around the theme of restless evangelicalism. Combining restlessness with evangelicalism has been the story of my adult life. I don't see how I could have survived in the evangelical movement without the freedom made possible by the restlessness.

And I see a marvelous kind of restlessness in evangelicalism's younger generation. I continue to teach seminary students, and I regularly do visits to Christian colleges and university student ministries. I am grateful for what I see in this generation.

At a gathering of evangelical seminary leaders, a dozen or so of us were discussing trends on our respective campuses. One president complained that too many students in his school were entering their programs of study without a clear commitment to pastoral ministry. "They're just trying to 'explore options' in seminary," he said. "This is not good! We need men"—his school did not encourage women to pursue ordained ministries—"who are passionate about standing in the pulpit and preaching the Word!"

Another president challenged him: "I'm actually impressed with this generation of seminary students. They see more complexities than we did when we went to seminary. Many of them have traveled internationally. They are concerned about poverty, homeless kids, sex trafficking. They worry about racism and the economic divide here in North America. They care deeply about being good stewards of the creation. And they have a heart for reaching the lost with a vibrant Christian message. If they feel compelled to 'explore options,' it is because they have a big vision of what it means to serve the kingdom—and they're not sure that a pulpit-centered ministry is the best place for them to serve the Lord. They are looking for where they can fit in effectively in the kingdom!"

He had it right, as I see things. Many of the students whom I spend time with—graduate and undergraduate—are restless in their evangelicalism. I am deeply grateful for that.

My own evangelical restlessness started for me in my early teens. I worked one summer in the kitchen crew at a fundamentalist Bible conference. One of the older workers was a college student with strong intellectual interests. I enjoyed talking to him about things he was interested in, even though I did not always understand what he was saying. But when he told me about a book he was reading about faith and science, I asked if I could see it. The book was *A Christian View of Science and the Scripture* by Bernard Ramm.

He lent the book to me with the warning that I was not to let anyone else at the Bible conference see it. The author, he said, argued that scientific evolution was not as bad a viewpoint as the folks at our Bible conference thought it was. This meant that the book had stirred up some controversy in the evangelical world.

Ramm's book was a breath of fresh air for me. I had just taken a biology course in high school, where the teacher said positive things about evolution. What she said made sense to me, but I was constantly warned by preachers and teachers in my Christian circles that we were in a battle against that kind of perspective. I wasn't convinced by their warnings, and reading

Ramm gave me some hope that I could entertain my misgivings without feeling that I was giving up the biblical faith as such. My friend reassured me in this regard. Ramm, he said, was an evangelical, and that was a good thing. It meant that he believed the gospel. But he was not a fundamentalist, like the folks at the Bible conference where we were working. I was not very clear about the distinction he was making, but being an evangelical struck me as a very good thing.

A year or so later, I was to encounter the "evangelical" label again. And this time, looking back on the occasion from the distance of over a half century, it was an encounter that helped to set the course for the rest of my spiritual and theological journey.[1]

It was in October 1956, and I—a sixteen-year-old—was home alone when the very first issue of *Christianity Today* arrived in our mailbox. My dad was a pastor, and in its earliest years the magazine was sent free to clergy. As I sorted the day's mail, I glanced over the new magazine's cover. Seeing that there was an article by Billy Graham inside, I sat down to read what he had to say about the authority of the Bible.

Having gotten into the magazine, I also read the editorial, "Why *Christianity Today*?," by Carl F. H. Henry. I knew nothing about Henry, nor was I clued in to—except for what my Bible conference friend had told me about Bernard Ramm—the complexities of discussions about evangelical identity. When Henry referred to the need for evangelical scholarship, however, as well as to the importance of supporting a network of evangelical scholars working in various academic settings around the world, I had a clear sense that this was a different kind of voice than those I was accustomed to hearing in my present spiritual environs.

1. The following section is adapted from Richard J. Mouw, "Happy Birthday, Christianity Today!," *First Things*, October 17, 2016, https://www.firstthings.com/blogs/firstthoughts/2016/10/happy-birthday-christianity-today. Used with permission.

I doubt that I had ever before come across a serious call for a coupling of "evangelical" and "scholarship." I'm not sure that I had even heard any encouraging words about the need for Christians to engage in careful *thinking*. The evangelicalism of my youth was heavy on anti-intellectualism. Sometimes it took an overtly mocking form. In my childhood, for example, I could not have given any kind of definition of the word "exegesis," but I could have told you that whatever it was, it was something that true Christians avoid at all costs. I had learned that from a traveling revival preacher who had proclaimed that, in contrast to what he had learned in the few seminary courses he had taken, "you don't need exegesis, you just need Jesus!"

More often, though, it was a steady stream of warnings against placing too much of an emphasis on the life of the mind. If someone—a college professor, for example—was held up as a person to be admired, it was typically because he or she was "strong in the faith" in spite of a record of academic accomplishments.

In reading that first issue of *Christianity Today*, then, I had the clear sense that Carl Henry was trying to tell us something different. And in my teenage heart I felt that by responding favorably to what he was saying, I was engaging in a bit of a rebellion—not unlike what I experienced in reading Ramm— against the kind of evangelicalism that had shaped me thus far.

My feeling of harboring a guilty pleasure in absorbing what Henry had to say, though, was held in check by the fact that Billy Graham was somehow allied with all of this. He was a hero of mine, and that would only intensify in the next year. In 1957 he would begin his crusade in New York City's Madison Square Garden, and folks from our northern New Jersey congregation sponsored bus trips into the big city to attend those meetings. On one of those evenings I had invited some of my non-Christian high school friends to attend with us, and when one of them moved down the aisle in response to Billy Graham's invitation to join hundreds of others in making a public commitment to Jesus Christ as Lord and Savior, I made the trek also. For me on that night, it was a public witness to the fact that I embraced the promises of the gospel. And Graham's obvious partnership with Carl Henry at *Christianity Today* assured me that I did not have to choose between the evangelist's call to a personal commitment to Christ and a serious engagement in the life of the mind. Or, as I would later come to see, between evangelicalism and serious engagement with the issues of public life.

| 4 |

Toward a Second Naivete

David Allan Hubbard, my predecessor in the Fuller presidency, liked to quote Oliver Wendell Holmes: "I would not give a fig for the simplicity this side of complexity, but I would give my life for the simplicity on the other side of complexity." That is a nice way of stating what the philosopher Paul Ricoeur meant by his distinction between "the first naivete" and "the second naivete." To be naive in the first sense is to hold to a certain viewpoint in a precritical manner. The second kind of naivete is postcritical. It is a state of mind that one has *come to* by means of critical examination and reflection.

For me, the most important part of my journey toward the second naivete pertains to my views on the Bible's authority. It was restlessness that moved me beyond the first naivete, but my restlessness brought me to a new way of affirming what I had been taught about the Bible's authority.

When I worked at the fundamentalist Bible conference that I described earlier, we were very sure about the Bible's authority.

We would express our confidence with statements of this sort: "If the Bible says it, then I believe it."

I have come a long way since then in my understanding of how the Bible is meant to function in Christian life and thought. And here is how I would put it now: "If the Bible says it, then I believe it."

Yes, the same affirmation. I really don't have any reservations about putting my trust in the Bible's supreme authority using the words of my youth. But many times in the intervening six decades I have worked hard to sustain that confidence. And these days I don't so much see myself as going back to that early mode of certainty—rather, I have gone forward to developing that certainty in a new way.

This is really, I think, what was going on with Karl Barth when a journalist, during Barth's visit to the United States in the early 1960s, asked the great theologian how he would set forth the basic intent of his theology in a few words. Barth's answer: "Jesus loves me, this I know, for the Bible tells me so."

What is so charming about Barth's answer is the way he uses what is rightly viewed as an expression of a rather simple childlike faith to summarize what he has arrived at in his own very sophisticated exposition of Christian thought. He was not engaging in spiritual or theological regression. He was not saying that, in spite of his complex theological journey through the years, he could go back to where he began his journey as a child. Rather, he was telling us where he had arrived as a *result* of his complicated theological pilgrimage.

Barth was giving expression to a second naivete when asked about his theology. And while I surely fall far short of Karl Barth's level of theological acumen, I can offer a similar "second naivete" version of "If the Bible says it, then I believe it."

| The "Tumult of Opinions"[1]

A big problem, of course, is getting clear about what the Bible really *says* on some important topics. I experienced considerable confusion on this subject during my upbringing. My father supported infant baptism, and often at family gatherings he and his brother, a Baptist preacher, would engage in lengthy arguments about the subject. They would each quote Scripture, but neither was able to convince the other. I found this worrisome. And there were other arguments that I was aware of in my childhood. Predestination or free will? Tongues speaking for the present age? A millennium that is yet to come, prior to the battle of Armageddon? Were all my Catholic friends going to hell?

Right around the time when I turned thirteen, our family traveled across the country from New York State to California. We stopped off in Salt Lake City to do the Tabernacle tour. We were given a pamphlet with the title, "Joseph Smith Tells His Own Story"—the founder of Mormonism's account of his "First Vision." My parents considered what we had experienced in our Utah venture to be an encounter with clever anti-Christian propaganda. But as I sat reading Joseph Smith's story in the back-seat of our car, I was taken with his report of his own confusions in his youth about the religious disputes that raged in his hometown of Palmyra, New York: Presbyterians were arguing with Baptists, and each of them attacked the views of the Methodists. "In the midst of this war of words and tumult of opinions," Smith reports, "I often said to myself, what is to be done? Who of all these parties are right; or, are they all wrong together? If any one of them be right, which is it, and how shall I know it?"[2]

1. Parts of this section are adapted from Richard J. Mouw, *Talking with Mormons: An Invitation to Evangelicals* (Grand Rapids: Eerdmans, 2012), 5–7. Used with permission.

2. The Joseph Smith Papers, "History, circa June 1839–circa 1841 [Draft 2]," 2018, http://www.josephsmithpapers.org/paper-summary/history-circa-june-1839-circa-1841-draft-2/2.

I was not about to follow in the religious direction that Smith went, but he captured nicely at that point my own confused state of mind as a thirteen-year-old.

When I was a graduate student in the Philosophy Department at the University of Chicago, I would often ask my fellow students what questions or interests in their lives motivated them to study philosophy. I got several different kinds of answers. For some it was simply the love of logical clarity that they found in analytic philosophy. For others it was early faith and reason concerns. Several talked about trying to find meaning. One friend told me that already as a child he had puzzled much about "the One and the Many."

It has often occurred to me that reading Smith in the backseat of our family car identified for me the question that eventually led me into philosophical studies: How do we decide between conflicting—but seemingly coherent—perspectives on important topics? Recently I wrote a memoir-type book on what I depicted as a "lifelong quest for common ground."[3] That topic of commonness has certainly been the underlying theme of just about all the serious intellectual work in which I have engaged. But it is directly linked to the question of whether there is some place to stand, intellectually and spiritually, that allows us to see how to adjudicate what seem like irreconcilable differences in beliefs and practices.

| Learning Hermeneutics

My early puzzles along these lines focused in good part on how to understand what the Bible actually teaches. My deep interest in that subject never motivated me to become a biblical scholar

3. Richard J. Mouw, *Adventures in Evangelical Civility: A Lifelong Quest for Common Ground* (Grand Rapids: Brazos, 2016).

as such. But questions about hermeneutics and authority have loomed large for me in my journey from the first naivete to the second.

A book that I read in my senior year of college made a deep impression on me in setting the direction that I would take in my journey of reflecting on biblical matters. I read Edward John Carnell's *Case for Orthodox Theology* shortly after it appeared in 1959. The president of our college was a scholar of a very conservative bent, and he would often use his chapel talks to issue warnings against books that he worried might influence us. When he told us that Carnell had written a very dangerous book, falsely claiming to be making a case for orthodox theology, several of us ordered copies of the book and read what Carnell had to say.

The passages my friends and I enjoyed most at the time were the ones where Carnell portrayed the fundamentalist movement as *"orthodoxy gone cultic."*[4] He was especially biting in his critique of fundamentalism's "negative ethic." Fundamentalists, Carnell said, make much of what they see as the evils of the use of alcohol, playing cards, dancing, and theater attendance, which allows them to "divert attention from grosser sins— anger, jealousy, hatred, gossip, lust, idleness, malice, backbiting, schism, guile, injustice—and every shade of illicit pride."[5]

That was fun to read, and it did reinforce the sense that fundamentalism did not need to define the standards of biblical orthodoxy for me. What had the lasting impact for me from Carnell's book, however, was his discussion of hermeneutics. I have read much more technical treatments of the subject since then, but my basic perspective is still what I learned from Carnell's brief treatment. He began by emphasizing the way the

4. Edward John Carnell, *The Case for Orthodox Theology* (Philadelphia: Westminster, 1959), 113 (italics in the original).
5. Carnell, *Case for Orthodox Theology*, 120.

Bible sets forth a pattern of "progressive revelation," followed by the principles set forth under these five headings: "*first*, the New Testament interprets the Old Testament; *secondly*, the Epistles interpret the Gospels; *thirdly*, systematic passages interpret the incidental; *fourthly*, universal passages interpret the local; *fifthly*, didactic passages interpret the symbolic."[6] Those guidelines are simply stated, and they have served me well in my understanding of biblical orthodoxy.

Biblical Affirmations

Here is a story that I have heard several times, about how the consensus statement on biblical authority was decided by the evangelicals who gathered in Lausanne, Switzerland, in the summer of 1974 (I was not there) for the International Congress on World Evangelism. All the participants agreed on the basic concern that brought them together. They were firmly convinced that evangelism is a high priority for the mission of the global church. They disagreed on some other things, such as on the relationship between evangelism and social action and some other long-standing theological hot-button issues for evangelicals. In the drafting of the Lausanne Covenant, though, much of this was settled amicably by the formulation of carefully worded consensus statements.

What to say about biblical authority, however, was problematic. While the debate over "inerrancy" would heat up in the next couple of years with the 1976 publication of Harold Lindsell's blockbuster *The Battle for the Bible*, the tensions were already in the air at Lausanne. Some of the more conservative participants wanted a statement on the subject that would exclude the views of many others who were gathered

6. Carnell, *Case for Orthodox Theology*, 52–53 (italics in the original).

there. It looked like the debate would end in a failure to find a consensus statement on this topic. Then John Stott proposed a formulation: that the Bible is "without error in all that it affirms." No one could find fault with this, and it was endorsed by the assembly.

Later on, of course, some of those more conservative folks had second thoughts (although not in time to change the final wording). They realized that "affirms" is a fairly loose term. You can say (as I would) that while Genesis 1 uses the language of "days" of creation, it does not mean to *affirm* that the world was created in six literal days—just as the fact that the Bible uses "four corners of the earth" language (Rev. 7:1) does not mean that it *affirms* that the earth is square. What the Bible "affirms" is something to be decided by looking at a variety of factors—context, author's intent, connections to other things that are taught in the Scriptures, and so on. The Lausanne Covenant allows us to acknowledge these complexities while still using the term "inerrant."

Why even use that word, though? Many of my evangelical friends believe it must simply be abandoned because of the divisive results of the "battle for the Bible" that was waged in recent decades. I have some sympathy for that assessment, although the debate that raged in the wake of Lindsell's book is in many ways a misguided argument. For example, while "inerrant" is not a very popular word with some of my Fuller colleagues, those same folks would never tolerate anyone in their midst saying that the Bible is simply wrong about some teaching. Our theological discussions at Fuller take it for granted that our views must be brought into conformity to the teachings of the Scriptures.[7]

7. I discuss this further in my book, *The Smell of Sawdust: What Evangelicals Can Learn from Their Fundamentalist Heritage* (Grand Rapids: Zondervan, 2000).

The debate over inerrancy functioned as a political skirmish within the evangelical movement. It was an attempt to draw the boundaries that mark out evangelical identity in a restrictive manner. The arguments were more about methods of studying the Scriptures than they were about whether the Bible contains errors. The underlying question was whether we evangelicals are open to new ways of deciding *what* the Bible teaches. As A. W. Tozer was fond of putting it: we can use all kinds of tools and methods for getting at the meaning of the Scriptures, but once the meaning is discovered, it trumps all other claims on the subject.

One of the periodicals that came into our home during my teenage years was *The Sword of the Lord*, edited by the Southern evangelist John R. Rice. Its style was, to put it mildly, confrontational and abrasive—later I learned that some evangelicals gave it the nickname "The Knife of the Spirit." Rice regularly attacked Billy Graham for compromising with liberals, and he was hostile toward the larger "neoevangelical" movement for what he saw as its apostate tendencies.

A one-frame *Sword of the Lord* cartoon stands out in my memory. It was a courtroom scene. The judge, sitting on a high bench, was labeled "The Word of God." Several men were lined up to take the witness stand: I know that one was "Liberal" and another was "Neoevangelical"; I think that "Roman Catholic" and "Neoorthodox" were also in the lineup. Another man, probably a clerk, was addressing the bench. His words: "But, Your Honor, these men want to put *you* on trial!"

This was the concern that surfaced in the later battle for the Bible—the worry that many scholars in the evangelical world were joining the biblical critics in a project of calling the authority of God's Word into question. That concern—at least as it applies to the theologians with whom I work—is based on a confusion. When the use of new critical tools is harnessed to a deep devotion to the Bible as an utterly reliable word from God, the results can greatly enrich our understanding of God's will for our lives.

Prominent in the arsenal of the battlers for the Bible has been the slippery-slope argument—that these new methods of biblical study will inevitably weaken our commitment to key evangelical teachings and emphases. I see no evidence that this prediction was a sound one.

But, for all of that, I still like the word "inerrant." It says something that is not captured by, say, "infallible." The Bible does indeed present us with a *message* that is to be believed by us. To be sure, the Bible is more than a set of propositions that require our cognitive assent. It gives us prayers, dreams, visions, commands, songs, complaints, pleadings, parables, love letters—"inerrant" isn't exactly the right word for explaining how these elements of the biblical record ought to be guiding us in our lives. But the Bible is not *less* than a message from the living God, a message that contains *truths* that we must hold on to for our very lives. How we respond to what the Bible tells us about God's dealings with humankind is a matter of eternal significance. So, again, with all the proper nuances, I can still say, "If the Bible says it, then I believe it."

In my senior year of college I also read James Packer's *Fundamentalism and the Word of God,* and that set the course of my thinking about biblical authority as such. The Christian has to choose, Packer writes, among three options. Our basic authoritative reference point is either the Bible, the church, or human experience. I agreed with Packer that it has to be the Bible, and I have never wavered from that fundamental conviction. So, yes, I can say with the folks at the Bible conference: "If the Bible says it, then I believe it." But again, the big issue, of course, is getting clear about what the Bible, in what it is "saying," actually *affirms*.

| 5 |

Remembering

In a lecture I was giving to a large student audience at an evangelical college, I mentioned the name of Billy Graham. I just mentioned him in passing, with no sense that I needed to explain to whom I was referring.

In a conversation later that day a faculty member on that campus told me something that took me by surprise. She was lecturing in one of her classes, she said, and like me she mentioned Billy Graham in passing. After class a student came up to her and asked who this Billy Graham person was. In the next class session she asked the students to raise their hands if they knew anything about Billy Graham. In a class of forty, she said, only about six students raised their hands.

I was taken aback. I could imagine that response in a classroom at a state university. But at this school? There had been a time of worship before the lecture I had given to the student body that day, and it had been fifteen minutes of the enthusiastic worship of Jesus, with hundreds of outstretched arms raised in fervent praise to the Lord. Afterward a student approached me with a question about a Scripture verse that he showed me in his much underlined Bible. Another student wanted to tell me about her efforts when, as a high school student, she witnessed to her "unsaved friends."

I had no question that on this campus I was in evangelical territory. Yet most of the students knew little or nothing about Billy Graham. Rob Bell, yes, and even Tony Campolo. But not Billy Graham.

Earlier in this book I listed a few of the saints and heroes of my evangelical upbringing (see chapter 1 under the heading "Still Viable?"). For any twenty-year-olds who might have read that list, I might as well have been naming the teenagers I once met in a Haitian village.

I now am aware of this. And in retrospect I should not have been surprised about the unfamiliarity of Billy Graham. He was an evangelical icon in my life, and as I write this I grieve his passing. But for a present twenty-year-old evangelical, Billy Graham had been pretty much invisible—bedridden in North Carolina—for much of that person's life.

It would be wonderful if this generation had the kind of knowledge of Billy Graham that I do. Reading my friend Grant Wacker's wonderful biography, *America's Pastor: Billy Graham and the Shaping of a Nation*, would be a great start. But the issue here is not about this or that saint or hero of the past. It is about a sense of being connected to the past.

| Historical Grounding

I talked once with a young man in his thirties who had already made his mark in Silicon Valley, having been involved in a few start-ups that had done well. He wanted to talk about church history with me, and I was surprised about how much he knew about medieval Christianity. "I spend a lot of time reading about the twelfth century," he told me.

I asked him why he chose that century, and he said that he had taken a course on medieval thought in his university studies, and a couple of people and events in the twelfth century had caught his interest. Later, after he was actively engaged in the high-tech world, he decided to make a hobby of immersing himself in learning more about that century. And then he made this intriguing comment: "In Silicon Valley we are always moving quickly—and it is always skimming over surfaces. I feel the need to be *grounded* in something. So I chose the twelfth century!"

One of the comments about Christian higher education that I have used in speaking and writing on the subject is by Craig Dykstra, former vice president of the Lilly Endowment and now a professor at Duke University. Dykstra, speaking to a group of faculty from church-related colleges, emphasized the need to form students "who see deeply into the reality of things and who love that reality—over time and across circumstances."[1] My Silicon Valley friend was making the same point in concrete detail.

That kind of awareness is important for our evangelical movement as such. A team of sociologists headed up by Robert Bellah argues that healthy nations must be "communities of memory"—and the same applies to other social units.[2] We evangelicals have inherited much from believers who "over time and across circumstances" have been faithful to the gospel. When we fail to nurture those memories we can easily get caught up in "skimming over surfaces."

1. Craig Dykstra, "Communities of Conviction and the Liberal Arts," *The Council of Societies for the Study of Religion Bulletin* 19, no. 3 (September 1990): 62.
2. Robert Bellah et al., *Habits of the Heart: Individualism and Commitment in American Life* (Los Angeles: University of California Press, 1985), 152–54.

| Learning from the Past

I know that the lessons of history are often overrated. But they frequently do serve us well in very practical ways.

A Fuller student told me that the class he was taking from me was the final course of his seminary program. I asked him what was next for him, and he told me that he and his wife were going to "do a church plant." And then he added quickly that they were not going to be affiliated with any denomination. "We're stepping out in faith—on our own," he said.

His tone was rather emphatic, so I pushed him as to why he and his wife were choosing not to affiliate with a denomination. He told me that he had started seminary with the intention of serving the denomination in which he was raised—he named it—but he had come to see that church as "too restrictive" about congregational ministries: "My wife and I want to be led by the Spirit and not by a church bureaucracy!"

We had some time to talk, so I asked him whether he knew much about the history of the denomination he was leaving behind. He did not. So I told him what I knew. That denomination has its origins in early eighteenth-century Europe. It was a time when the worship services in the established Protestant congregations—meeting in former Catholic cathedrals—were quite formal liturgically, and the sermons often were lengthy discourses on specific points of doctrine. Many believers decided to supplement those services with smaller groups of Christians meeting in private homes for Bible study and prayer. Eventually they came to rely completely on these fellowships for their spiritual nurture, completely avoiding the worship in the formal churches.

The folks who emigrated to North America in the next century continued these house church practices for a while. But they also sought out like-minded groups elsewhere, and cooperated in leadership training and the sponsoring of missionaries. As the local groups grew in size, they established church buildings. Eventually their connections with one another developed into what is today a major denomination.

I don't think my brief historical account persuaded the young couple to renew their denominational ties, but they did see my basic point. There is a real possibility that what they would be establishing would eventually—maybe a couple of generations down the line—look a lot like what they were presently leaving behind.

I could offer a similar narrative regarding seminary education. In my own Dutch Reformed tradition, education for pastoral ministry began as on-the-job training. In the early days of Calvinism in the Netherlands, candidates for ordination would work and study under the supervision of an older pastor in a local congregation. After a while, however, the responsibilities for this education came to be shared with other pastors in the region. A minister in one town might be more skilled in biblical languages and would accept responsibility for mentoring younger candidates from other congregations. This kind of curricular specialization soon spread. Finally, the distribution of labor led to establishing schools where full-time faculty took over the tasks.

I think about this history these days when I hear some megachurch pastors talk about "training our own" in the context of the local congregation rather than sending candidates for ministry off to seminary campuses. Not that I am convinced that an evolution in the direction of seminary campuses is inevitable. But it is at least important to be aware of this history, and of the factors that gradually necessitated some kind of shared programs of theological training. In our own time, of course, this new distribution of labor could well be shaped by social media and newer information technologies. But the memories of how things have gone in the past make me a bit concerned when I hear a senior pastor say about a young man whom he has designated as a future pastoral leader in his congregation: "I can teach him all he needs to know about what it means to be a minister."

Or, for a slightly different narrative, one can look at the history of "Bible schools" in North America, which were often founded as vital alternatives to the established theological schools. A good case in point is Gordon Bible Institute, founded in 1889 by A. J. Gordon, who complained that "our Protestant ministry today" was becoming "impoverished by excess of learning." He was "perpetually chagrined," Gordon testified, "to see how much better many of the unschooled lay preachers of our time can handle the Scriptures than many clergymen who have passed through the theological curriculum."[3]

For almost a century the kind of school Gordon envisioned provided "practical training" programs that were characterized by—to use Virginia Brereton's apt characterization in her excellent book on the history of the Bible school movement— "brevity, practicality and efficiency."[4] All of this had a profound impact on the ethos of the evangelical movement. And the impact offered many gifts. For one thing, the Bible schools educated thousands of women for leadership in (nonordained) ministry roles.

While we still have some of the older style Bible schools in our midst, many of them—most notably the ones founded by A. J. Gordon and Dwight L. Moody, along with the Bible Institute of Los Angeles (BIOLA)—have become accredited

3. Ernest B. Gordon, *Adoniram Judson Gordon: A Biography, with Letters and Illustrative Extracts Drawn from Unpublished or Uncollected Sermons and Addresses* (New York: Revell, 1896), 171–72.

4. Virginia Brereton, *Training God's Army: The American Bible School, 1880–1940* (Bloomington: University of Indiana Press, 1990), 62.

seminaries characterized by a broad curriculum and solid teaching and scholarship.

Again, I am not advocating an inevitability thesis here. We can certainly think of cultural contexts today where the "practical training" school can contribute much to leadership education for the church. But anyone who wants to insist that this is the only viable form of education for church leadership should at least be informed by the history of the Bible institute movement.

| Memory and Forgetting

In insisting that it is good to remember some of the specifics of our evangelical histories, I know that I run the risk of getting caught up in nostalgia. I recognize that risk in myself, and I do not want to let it guide my thinking. I have been a pretty unhappy evangelical at various points of my life. There are no good old days to which I want us to return. I do have people in my evangelical past who serve as inspiring models for me of clear and courageous faith. But there are also many who have provided me with examples of how *not* to act and think as Christians. We learn much also from the bad memories.

At a theological conference, we were discussing the spiritual challenges of dealing with painful pasts. A black theologian from South Africa talked about his struggles with remembering what it was like to live under the horrors of the apartheid era while also wanting to move toward the future with a profound sense of Christian hope. He told a story about an African child whose teacher asked her to define "memory." After thinking about it, the child said, "Memory is that thing that helps me to forget." The theologian saw that as profound. Having a healthy memory, he said, also means knowing what we need to forget in order not to be consumed by a spirit of bitterness.

I know many people—some of them are close friends—who
have been deeply hurt by evangelicalism. They live with bit-
ter memories of abusive leaders, cultural prejudices, narrow-
minded thinking, and more. I saw much of that myself, but I
was never seriously wounded by it. My personal lack of bitterness about evangelicalism's negative features has nothing to
do with any virtue on my part. In fact, it may have to do with
some less-than-noble factors.

I have often reflected in this regard on a comment that the
well-known historian Jaroslav Pelikan made when he was interviewed by Mark Noll in 1990 for *Christianity Today*. Noll
asked the noted Lutheran scholar—Pelikan later moved on to
Orthodoxy—to compare his time of teaching at Valparaiso
University, a Lutheran school, with his later years on the faculty
at Yale. Pelikan was not kind about church-related academic
institutions. The best way to serve the Christian community,
he said, was to work at a secular institution. When you are in
the church's employ, Pelikan explained, "you have to give the
church what it needs, not what it wants. And in order to do
that you have to leave its payroll."[5]

I was irritated by this comment when I first read it. My in-
stinctive response was that Pelikan was not being fair to people
like me. I have spent my academic career on evangelicalism's
"payroll," and I have tried to contribute to what the movement
needs, rather than simply giving it what it wants.

That was my immediate response—but it was too quick. I
have to acknowledge the temptations that come with a position of privilege in a given community. A middle-aged woman
pastor whom I recently met wanted nothing to do with the
evangelicalism of her upbringing. As a thirteen-year-old she

5. Mark A. Noll, "The Doctrine Doctor," interview with Jaroslav Pelikan,
Christianity Today 34, no. 12 (September 10, 1990): 26.

was ostracized for challenging her Sunday school teacher's attack on "evolutionism," and then she was later scorned for asking the folks in her church why she, as a bright high school senior, could not think about studying to become an ordained pastor. These experiences were the end of the line for her with evangelicalism. Having nothing to compensate for the sense of rejection she experienced, she quietly resigned from the evangelical movement, seeking other spiritual and intellectual paths. For her, the very word "evangelical" evokes painful memories.

I have to be careful in how I make my case to folks like her. Whatever bad experiences I may have had growing up evangelical, they have been more than outweighed by the rewards I have had from being kept on evangelicalism's "payroll." A liberal churchman once asked me, "How does a person like you survive in evangelicalism?" I gave a polite answer, but what I felt like saying was, "Duh! Survive? As the president of a large and influential evangelical institution, I basically get *rewarded* for being an evangelical!"

When I think about that response—and it was a fairly accurate one—I realize that I was actually expressing a reason for taking a critical look at my own motives. Suppose I carried the kinds of wounds that the woman pastor bears—of being scorned by evangelicals who were important in my life. Would the evangelical convictions that I celebrate have survived that kind of treatment? Asking that question in an honest spirit has not led me to question my basic evangelical convictions. But it does keep me aware that for me those convictions are connected to being in a position of privilege in the evangelical movement.

The African child's definition of memory, then, comes to me as a serious spiritual assignment: "Memory is that thing that helps me to forget." In highlighting what I see as the good things in the evangelical heritage, am I forgetting to pay attention to the bad things? Have I given enough attention to the deep wounds of those who have suffered at the hands of my community? Do I have any healing words for them about what a healthy memory of their own painful past should help them to forget—and even to assist them in remembering some things that can still bring good news to their souls?

In making my case for evangelicalism in these pages, I may not succeed fully in fulfilling that assignment. But I do keep reminding myself of the weight of the obligation to do so. No legitimate defense of evangelicalism can avoid acknowledging that obligation.

I need to repeat the distinction I made at the beginning of this book, though. I am not saying that we should hang on to the "evangelical" label at all costs. But I do want to hold on to the good things that have characterized the evangelicalism of the past. It is important for us to keep working at being—to reiterate the wonderful phrase from Robert Bellah—"communities of memory."

| 6 |

Being Clear about Sin

In the fall of 1975 I received a letter from Paul Vitz, a psychology professor at New York University (NYU), asking whether I ever had occasion to visit New York City. He had read something I had written and was interested in getting together to talk about mutual interests. It so happened that I was on leave from Calvin College that year, serving as a postdoctoral fellow in the Princeton University Sociology Department. New York City was only a short train ride away, so it was not long before we met for lunch in Greenwich Village.

Vitz began our time together by telling me that he felt awkward about talking with me. He was a tenured professor at NYU, but had only recently become a Christian, and he was just beginning to work out what his newfound faith meant for his intellectual pursuits. I was one of the first Christian scholars he was reaching out to.

We had a great conversation. It was clear to me that he was on his way to becoming a creative Christian scholar. When our time together came to an end, he quite apologetically asked whether I would take a look at the draft of an essay he had written. I read it on the train back to Princeton and was deeply impressed by his exploration of how a biblically grounded view of "dying unto self" in committing one's whole being to God stood in sharp contrast to the various "self-actualization" perspectives (Gestalt therapy, Sartrean existentialism, etc.) that had previously shaped Vitz's thought. I immediately contacted my friends at Eerdmans Publishing Company in Grand Rapids, urging them to contact him about expanding the essay into a book. Vitz's *Psychology as Religion: The Cult of Self-Worship* appeared in print two years later.

Around the time that his book was published, I arranged for Vitz to give a lecture at Calvin College. A sizable audience was present, including several psychologists, psychiatrists, and social workers from Pine Rest Christian Hospital, an excellent psychiatric hospital founded by the Dutch Reformed community.

Vitz skillfully presented his views about selfhood. The point of our lives as humans, he argued, is not to develop a positive view of our potential. We are sinners who need to be called into an obedient relationship to God. We need to lose our sinful selves in order to find our redeemed selves. These emphases, he insisted, have clear implications for how we promote human well-being in counseling and therapy.

I was a bit taken aback by the criticisms of many in the audience, especially from those working actively in mental health services. These were good Calvinists, and none of them were inclined to challenge the basics of Vitz's theology. But many of the clients they were ministering to in the Reformed community, they testified, were not caught up in quests for "self-actualization." These mental health workers had seen the psychological effects for Christians who were brought up on messages about being depraved sinners who live their lives under a sense of divine judgment. For these professionals, drawing on biblical resources for restoring a positive self-image in their clients was an important step toward healthy human flourishing.

This was a lesson in contextualization for me. Paul Vitz certainly was on target in his critique of the self-actualization culture. But the Calvinist mental health professionals were issuing important insights into how a certain way of dwelling on guilty selfhood can be inimical to spiritual flourishing.

| Worms and Wanderers[1]

So, how do we get it right? I wish I had a clear answer on this. I see no alternative but to stay focused on the important theological issues, while also staying attentive to cultural factors. The Grand Rapids residents who grew up under a rather stern version of Calvinist orthodoxy needed to deal somewhat differently with the state of their souls than the folks who hung around in Greenwich Village coffee shops.

The theological bottom line on the sin question was stated succinctly for me in a powerful sermon that the nineteenth-century theologian Geerhardus Vos preached in the Princeton Seminary Chapel. His theme was "Seeking and Saving the Lost," and his text was Jesus's declaration in Luke 19:10 that "the Son of Man came to seek and to save the lost." Vos observed that to understand "the inherent logic of the structure of the gospel" is to be clear about the fact that when we dilute the meaning of the word "lost" we also end up diluting the

1. Parts of this section are adapted from Richard J. Mouw, "'Some Poor Sailor, Tempest Tossed': Nautical Rescue Themes in Evangelical Hymnody," in *Wonderful Words of Life: Hymns in American Protestant History and Theology*, ed. Richard J. Mouw and Mark A. Noll (Grand Rapids: Eerdmans, 2004), 242–44. Used with permission.

meaning of what it means "to save."[2] A reduced understanding of our sinful condition inevitably leads to a reduced Savior. That warning speaks to me in profound ways. The challenge, of course, is to explain the meaning of our "lostness" in a way that points us to the abundant grace that is made available to us through the Savior's redemptive work. But how we keep our sinfulness in perspective requires attention to the life situations of those whom we are attempting to lead to the Savior.

Attending seriously to life situations led, in the nineteenth century, to some toning down of harsh formulations about human sinfulness. Sandra Sizer tells this story in a compelling way in a fascinating book she wrote about evangelical hymnody in the nineteenth century. In the previous century, hymns often employed strongly condemnatory terms in describing the condition of the unregenerate sinner. A prime example is Isaac Watts's well-known line: "Would he devote that sacred head for such a worm as I?" Sizer comments, "The 'worm' is all the more despicable because he tries to exert his will against God, the ruler of all; that is, he is a *rebel* worm, a blasphemer, a criminal, a backslider, an upstart challenging God's rightful government; and such a worm deserves only to be damned."[3]

But then the nineteenth century saw a significant shift, with the increasing use of rescue themes. Now the hymns focused not so much on unregenerate people as arrogant rebels but on "these poor sinners," to use a phrase popular in that era. Evangelism meant reaching out to "the lost"—men and women who had wandered far from "home," with neither the strength nor the guidance to find the right path again. Many of the rescue hymns made use of nautical imagery about people drowning—such as

2. Geerhardus Vos, *Grace and Glory: Sermons Preached in the Chapel of Princeton Theological Seminary* (Edinburgh: Banner of Truth Trust, 1994), 56.
3. Sandra S. Sizer, *Gospel Hymns and Social Religion: The Rhetoric of Nineteenth-Century Religion* (Philadelphia: Temple University Press, 1978), 27.

"Throw Out the Lifeline" or "Let the Lower Lights Be Burning," with the lyric "Trim your feeble lamp, my brother. / Some poor sailor, tempest tossed, / trying hard to make the harbor, / in the darkness may be lost."

The evangelistic efforts being advocated with the use of that imagery expressed a serious degree of compassion for the unsaved person. And this in turn had to do with a new realization of the plight of sinners—especially those living in cities—who were caught up in difficult circumstances.

The evangelist Charles Crittendom is an interesting case in point in this regard. For a while his message to New York City prostitutes was that they should simply repent of their wicked ways and begin to walk the path of righteousness. He was soon overwhelmed, however, by the futility of his pleas: the women in question, he realized, were trapped in a way of life with no plausible alternatives. What was needed, then, were efforts to improve the social situation of these "fallen women." They could not simply turn their lives around by claiming the promises of the Gospels. They needed safe places to live during times of spiritual growth and training for new means of employment.

To be sure, the theology of "poor lost sinner" did not completely replace all that was associated with the "worm" depiction. Sizer acknowledges that the older elements of guilt, rebellion, and the need for pardon were still present in the rescue hymns. Nonetheless, she says, "the former scenario of a court of judgment is softer and more diffuse."[4] There seems to be an obvious reason for this softening. The evangelicals who were attempting to minister to the urban destitute, whose patterns of life were often in open conflict with biblical values, were able to see—in ways that previous generations of evangelicals had not found possible—that such folks were indeed locked into

4. Sizer, *Gospel Hymns and Social Religion*, 29.

structural-systemic factors that had to be taken into account in assessing the sinful patterns of urban life.

None of this was meant to minimize the rebellion elements in the sinful condition. Prostitution and drunkenness, for example, were still viewed as patterns of behavior that are displeasing to God. But these urban evangelists were unable to ignore the ways in which social conditions made it virtually impossible for many individuals *not* to fall into these sinful patterns. It was necessary, then, to view many sinful individuals as also people who were *victimized by* those societal patterns. Thus the drunkard and the prostitute could be viewed both as legal offenders *and* as persons deserving Christian compassion.

I see no need to choose between the two depictions. I still take what Sizer calls the "scenario of a court of judgment" seriously. When the apostle Paul says that "there is now no condemnation for those who are in Christ Jesus" (Rom. 8:1), he clearly implies that if we are *not* in Christ Jesus we stand condemned in the eyes of the divine Judge. Our condemned state made it necessary for Jesus, fully human and fully divine, to satisfy the demands of God's justice by paying the penalty for our shared rebellion.

| A Tender Call

Long before I joined the faculty at Fuller Theological Seminary, I was an admirer of Charles E. Fuller, the radio evangelist who founded the school. Listening to his *Old Fashioned Revival Hour* radio program was a weekly family event.

That Fuller held to a court of judgment theology—where condemned sinners are declared guilty but who are still offered God's merciful pardon—is beyond doubt. But his dominant approach to unbelievers was one of gentleness. When, at the conclusion of his weekly broadcast, he invited sinners to put their faith in Christ, it was with a pleading tone: "Won't you come? You have lost your way. You've wandered far from God. Jesus died for you. He wants to save you. Please come." And the choir would sing in the background: "Softly and tenderly Jesus is calling, . . . calling, 'O sinner, come home.'"

The "soft and tender" voice of the Savior in those pleas echoes what Sizer labels the "compassion" that came to dominate the urban evangelism of the nineteenth century. And I have no argument with that way of putting it. But I think the shift that occurred in the nineteenth century had to do with something that goes deeper than a compassionate spirit. It was the kind of shift that has taken place many times in the theological tradition over the centuries. We have focused on it in very explicit ways in recent decades: the *contextualization* of the gospel.

I will say more about contextualization later on. The basic recognition that our theological formulations are always embedded in a specific cultural context is fairly well established these days in the evangelical world. But it is too important for a discussion of the new opportunities for evangelicals simply to acknowledge its importance in passing. This is especially the case because seeing contextualization as important is directly related to our participation in a *global* evangelical movement. But having raised the topic of a theology of our sinful condition, I want to linger here with my focus on our North American context, saying some things about some present popularizers of the Christian message.

| Sin and Self-Image

Norman Vincent Peale's *Power of Positive Thinking* has been one of the big religious best sellers in American life. Its heyday was around the midpoint of the twentieth century, but it still manages to keep selling, with about five million copies presently in print. Around the time when the book was first published, Peale's ministry also founded *Guideposts* magazine, which presently has a circulation of about two million.

Claims about the late Dr. Peale's influence continue to be made. The late TV preacher Robert H. Schuller saw his own "possibility thinking" perspective as an updating of Peale's "positive thinking." Joel Osteen and the advocates of prosperity theology are also sometimes portrayed as following the general path that Peale walked.

I never met Norman Vincent Peale, but I did get to know his widow, Ruth Peale. I had some opportunities to talk with her at length when she attended some events at Fuller Seminary around the time she turned one hundred. Toward the end of the visit she said to me, "I wish Norman had gotten to know Fuller." Her husband, she said, felt rejected by theologians, especially after—these were her words—"that awful comment by Niebuhr." She was referring to a highly publicized remark by the Union Seminary theologian Reinhold Niebuhr, that "Paul is appealing, but Peale is appalling."

Then Mrs. Peale made an intriguing observation. "Norman really was an evangelical, you know! He liked to say that he was doing 'pre-evangelism,' and that he hoped that the people who became open to spiritual concerns through his influence would then hear Billy Graham preach the gospel and accept Christ."

I have often pondered that comment. I have some sympathy for how she portrayed her husband's intentions. And the sympathy was reinforced by a more substantive theological conversation about the ministry of Robert Schuller I had with a prominent theologian from the Netherlands: Hendrikus Berkhof, who taught for several decades at the University of Leiden.[5]

5. Parts of the following discussion on Robert Schuller are adapted from Richard J. Mouw, "Talking Calvinism with Robert H. Schuller," *First Things*, June

Berkhof has been one of my theological heroes. I had heard him lecture in my younger days, and I read many of his books with great interest. I had not met him personally, however, until a spring afternoon in 1990 when he visited Fuller Seminary. He had called my office to say that he was in Southern California and would like to visit Fuller. I arranged to give him a tour of the campus and then meet with him over lunch.

One of the first things I asked him was what he was doing on the American West Coast. "I just spent three days talking theology with Robert Schuller," he reported. He explained that Schuller had paid his way from the Netherlands just to spend some extended time exploring theological questions. The Canadian scholar Clark Pinnock was also a part of the conversation.

I was intrigued. I had gotten to know Schuller personally, and we had engaged in some theological conversation, but not of the extended sort that Berkhof had just had. I was eager to know what a prominent Dutch Reformed theologian would have to say about a TV preacher who was famous for his sermons on "possibility thinking" on his weekly *Hour of Power* program.

Schuller himself was trained in Reformed theology; when he and I met he would frequently recount how he had done a major project in seminary on John Calvin's *Institutes of the Christian Religion*. Schuller would tell me, though, that he purposely avoided referring to sin and guilt in his sermons, emphasizing more the importance of self-esteem.

Without clouding the discussion with my own impressions, I asked Berkhof about his impressions of Schuller's ministry, and his reply was memorable. Schuller had asked good questions, he said. And Berkhof was impressed by Schuller's sincerity in his efforts to find ways of bringing a Christian message of

---

2, 2015, https://www.firstthings.com/web-exclusives/2015/05/talking-calvinism
-with-robert-h-schuller. Used with permission.

hope into people's lives. It was clear, Berkhof said, that Schuller wanted to know what his two theologian guests had to say about the content of his preaching and writing.

"So," I asked Berkhof, "what did you tell him?" The Dutchman smiled and said: "In the end I told him, 'Schuller, your theology is like the first rocket phase of a space craft going to the moon. It gets the ship in the air, but pretty soon something else has to take over if the flight is to be successful!'"

That struck me as an insightful assessment of the overall theological character of Schuller's ministry. And I had some evidence that Schuller's theological "rocket" did indeed "get the ship in the air" on occasion. When I first arrived as a new faculty member at Fuller in the mid-1980s, I made a snide comment in a class lecture about Schuller's "possibility thinking" message. After class two students, both Latino men, came to the lectern and asked me not to make flippant comments about the ministry of the Crystal Cathedral. "We were drawn to the services there by the television program," they said. "That's where we came to a personal faith in Jesus Christ. We would not be studying for kingdom service at Fuller Seminary if it had not been for how the Lord used Robert Schuller in our lives."

| Addressing the Therapeutic Culture

In a conversation I had with Schuller after the Berkhof conversations, I told him that he was a gifted contextualizer of some of the principles of Reformed theology. He wasn't familiar with the term "contextualization," and he asked me to explain it. I told him that contextualizing the Christian message means taking a specific cultural context seriously. If I were going as a missionary to an animist village in an African country, I said, it would be important to prepare for my mission by studying animism and by reflecting on how to bring the biblical message to that village in a way that could be received as good news as I called animists to faith in Jesus Christ.

"You, Robert Schuller," I said, "have done precisely that for the popular therapeutic culture of Southern California. You have studied the context and found a way to speak to that context." He grinned broadly. "Yes, you have me right," he said. But the smile faded when I went on to say that I continued to have some questions whether he was properly contextualizing a Calvinist understanding of sin and grace in his efforts.

In reflecting on Professor Berkhof's use of the rocket imagery in assessing Schuller's approach, it has occurred to me that it was quite apt that Schuller's TV program was called the *Hour of Power*, and that Peale's book title proclaimed "the *power* of positive thinking." Initial bursts of energy, as Berkhof observed, are important for getting a journey started, even if something else needs to take over to get to the intended destination. I'm willing to live with the conviction that the kinds of "rockets" launched by Peale and Schuller can play a significant role in the larger mission of the kingdom.

| Health and Wealth

It probably would be wise now to move on to a different topic. Many of my evangelical friends—especially my academic peers—would not agree with my modest endorsement of the theologies of Peale and Schuller. But they might well—especially if they really are my friends!—see my endorsement as more or less harmless. I'm not likely to influence too many people on how I see "positive thinking" and "possibility thinking." And furthermore, both Peale and Schuller are no longer with us.

But I cannot avoid a question that quite likely has come up in the minds of some folks who have read what I just wrote: What about the prosperity gospel? Do I have a good word to say about that also? I don't know if I have a good word, but I am somewhat reluctant to utter nothing but bad words on the subject. So I will take a stab here at explaining my reluctance. I set forth the basics of my views on this subject in my 1994 book *Consulting the Faithful: What Christian Intellectuals Can Learn from Popular Religion*. I will highlight some of the points here.

On questions of how to assess popular religion from a theological perspective, I rely heavily on a fine essay, "The Flaw of the Excluded Middle," written by Paul Hiebert, who served as a missionary in India before teaching at Fuller Seminary and, after that, at Trinity Evangelical Divinity School.

Hiebert reports that he went to his assignment in India well equipped with two perspectives on the human condition. One was his "high" evangelical theology rooted in a biblical understanding of who we are as human beings and what God's creating and redeeming purposes are in the world. The other was—and Hiebert had been trained as an anthropologist—a scientific grasp of the nature of empirical reality.

In his missionary efforts, Hiebert did what he could to impart these insights to people in the rural villages where he ministered. There were evangelistic successes, as well as the implementing of educational programs. But he began to be aware of a "middle range" of concerns that he and his fellow missionaries were not addressing. This had to do with questions of this sort: How do I protect myself from injuries? What do I do when my child experiences a life-threatening illness that is not dealt with adequately by medical professionals? How do I deal with people who wish me harm? Where do I turn when I have no sufficient financial resources?

When Christian converts faced these very real situations, Hiebert says, they turned to the same place for help as their non-Christian neighbors: they went to shamans and diviners, people "who gave them definite answers, for these are the problems that loom large in their everyday life."[6]

What was missing here, Hiebert concludes, was an adequate theological framework for dealing with these "excluded middle" concerns. We have failed to develop, he argues, the kind of "holistic theology" that addresses the practical aspects of "divine guidance, provision and healing, of ancestors, spirits and invisible powers of this world, and of suffering, misfortune and death."[7]

| The "Middle Range" Agenda

The issues Hiebert was pointing to are important ones, and the prosperity preachers are addressing them directly. In the Majority World—Asia, Africa, Latin America—as well as in North America, these preachers have taken on the roles of the shamans and diviners to whom Hiebert's Indian converts turned in times of crisis. And it isn't enough simply to criticize them, without also acknowledging that our own theological academy has failed to address adequately the "middle range" that is so central to the message of prosperity preaching.

I still agree with what I propose in *Consulting the Faithful*. We need to do more work to develop a theology of "practical wisdom"—I use the Greek word for this, *phronēsis*—that takes these middle-range questions with utmost seriousness. To do this, I state, "requires a strategy that integrates various kinds of sensitivities and insights: theological, pastoral, ethical,

6. Paul G. Hiebert, "The Flaw of the Excluded Middle," *Missiology* 10 (1982): 45.
7. Hiebert, "Flaw of the Excluded Middle," 46.

spiritual, social scientific."[8] In proposing how to go about pursuing this strategy, I rely heavily on the importance of a proper Christian engagement with "the therapeutic." We need the kind of counseling, I argue, that equips Christian people to deal with the crises associated with grief, broken relationships, family systems, financial fears, and physical suffering.

In making my proposal, I offer what I label a "low-key compliment" to the prosperity preachers, because they are directly addressing these issues. But I also fault them for proclaiming a message that is lacking a serious grounding in "the high theological formulations of biblical truth."[9]

| "Once Delivered"

The big question these days, of course, is how much of what we have taken to be our high proclamations of biblical truth are themselves culturally conditioned. In one of my many conversations with my presidential predecessor, David Hubbard, he did a nice little exposition about the biblical mandate that we "should earnestly contend for the faith which was once delivered unto the saints" (Jude 3 KJV). Each of us had heard that King James phrasing used frequently in our respective evangelical upbringings. Hubbard said he still liked to quote it, but with several nuances in mind in these later years.

The notion that we contend for "*the* faith," he observed, has often been used to imply that God's will for us can be reduced to a simple formula or two. And that the Word was "once delivered" can ignore the important way in which the Spirit used many different human voices in bringing the Word

8. Richard J. Mouw, *Consulting the Faithful: What Christian Intellectuals Can Learn from Popular Religion* (Grand Rapids: Eerdmans, 1994), 54.
9. Mouw, *Consulting the Faithful*, 55–56.

to us—Hubbard cited Hebrews 1:1 here (again using the King James) that the Lord "at sundry times and in divers manners spake in time past unto the fathers by the prophets." And when we think of "the saints" today, he went on, we need to have a very diverse global community of believers in mind.

Hubbard was offering a "second naivete" affirmation of Jude's mandate. Each of his points is profoundly important. And the prosperity preachers have directed our attention to some issues we might otherwise miss on the third point. They have managed to touch the hearts of "the saints" in the Southern Hemisphere in a way that many of us in the Western theological academy have failed to grasp.

| 7 |

Our Deepest Yearnings

After receiving his theological education in both Japan and the United States, the theologian Kosuke Koyama was sent by his Japanese church as a young missionary to northern Thailand.[1] When he arrived there he experienced considerable culture shock. Thus far he had spent his time in urban settings, and now he found himself among people whose lives involved many days of standing in shallow water alongside water buffalo, to be followed by periods of attempting to stay dry during the onslaught of the monsoon rains.

In his book *Waterbuffalo Theology*, Koyama tells how he decided to spend some time reading the Bible as if he were standing alongside a water buffalo in a rice paddy. When he did so, passages and images leaped out at him that he had never really thought about before. He discovered that there is much in the Bible about water. God rules from a place above

1. Parts of the discussion about Kosuke Koyama are adapted from Richard J. Mouw, "Elected for a Global Mission," in *Reformed Mission in an Age of World Christianity*, ed. Shirley J. Roels (Grand Rapids: Calvin College Press, 2011), 17–18, 22–23. Used with permission.

the rains and the floods. God stays dry! These themes came to loom large in his presentation of the gospel to the people of northern Thailand.[2]

In reflecting on what he learned, Koyama uses what for me has been a compelling image. The missionary, he says, must always be aware of being "sandwiched between Christ's saving reality" and the "other-than-myself reality" of the neighbors to whom the gospel is being addressed. And this requires, he argues, engaging in two kinds of exegesis, or patterns of interpretation: the "exegesis of the Word of God and exegesis of the life and culture of the people among whom [the missionary] lives and works." This two-way exegesis—these two processes of interpretation—allows the missionary to take the questions asked in a given cultural context "to the enlightenment and judgment of the Word of God."[3]

That "sandwiched between" picture is helpful for understanding the church's mission in general. We are always in a specific culture, and as Christians we also need to be looking beyond our cultural context to God's revealed Word. And when we look to the Word for guidance, we must do so with the awareness that we are doing that interpretive looking, that exegesis, from a cultural context that influences both what questions and concerns we are bringing to the Word and how we hear that Word. And it helps to remember that, given that we are members of a Christian community, the gospel must be addressed to a rich variety of human cultural situations, speaking to those situations out of the complex and multifaceted storehouse of divine truth in God's Word.

There is nothing in this emphasis that undermines a commitment to biblical orthodoxy. But it does impress on us the need

2. Kosuke Koyama, *Waterbuffalo Theology* (Maryknoll, NY: Orbis, 1974), vii–viii, 32–40.
3. Koyama, *Waterbuffalo Theology*, 91.

to be conscious of how all of our preachings and theologizings are inevitably contextualized. None of us escapes the formative influence of our cultural situation in our understanding of the biblical message.

To recognize that the Bible's message is multifaceted helps to guard against a relativistic version of multiculturalism. God's Word speaks authoritatively to a variety of different cultural contexts, but it must not be seen as captured in a special way by any one of those contexts.[4]

So what we evangelicals have been learning—or at least what we should have been learning—from this kind of focus in recent decades is that all theology is contextualized. The plantation slave, the urban homemaker, the Russian peasant, the worker in a rice paddy, the tribal chief—each receives the gospel in terms of contextualized frameworks, questions, and anxieties. The awareness of this fact gives new occasions for celebrating the riches and the universality of the Christian gospel.

But for some of us there is also a word of judgment to be heard in this emphasis on contextualization. We have often been closed to other perspectives on the gospel. We have too quickly absolutized the cultural trappings that have accumulated around our understanding of the Christian faith. And this is especially unfortunate for those of us who are white Westerners, because we are, as a group, numbered among the rich and powerful of the earth; we consume a disproportionate amount of the world's goods. And many of us have a degree of control over our own destinies that would be unthinkable in other parts of the world. Unfortunately, this privileged position

4. The following discussion on cultural context is adapted from Richard J. Mouw, "Evangelicals and the Global Church," in *Worship, Tradition, and Engagement: Essays in Honor of Timothy George*, ed. David S. Dockery, James Earl Massey, and Robert Smith Jr. (Eugene, OR: Wipf and Stock, 2018), 353. Used by permission of Wipf and Stock publishers, https://www.wipfandstock.com.

has influenced the way in which we have received and understood the gospel. We have often filtered out crucial elements of the biblical message. We have often distorted the gospel so as to make it into a message with which we can live comfortably.

In saying these things, I am focusing primarily on North America. Since this is the cultural context I know best, it is the one I have thought most about. And that is the context I mean to be addressing in this book. But I do need to explain a bit about the more general theological perspective that guides me in this thinking about contemporary life in North America.

| "Hopes and Fears"[5]

In an oft-quoted passage from the beginning of his *Confessions*, Saint Augustine says in the form of a prayer: "Thou hast formed us for Thyself, and our hearts are restless till they find rest in Thee."[6] Augustine is expressing his conviction that our efforts to satisfy various needs and yearnings in our lives are driven by deeper spiritual needs that can be met only in a relationship with the living God.

It is also the perspective that C. S. Lewis illustrates in his typical compelling manner in one of his letters to his fictitious friend Malcolm. There Lewis refers to a rather serious argument that the two of them once had in Edinburgh—an encounter, Lewis says, where "we nearly came to blows."[7] Their heated argument was about the relationship between our rather

5. Parts of this section are adapted from Richard J. Mouw, "Surprised by Calvin," *First Things*, March 2009, https://www.firstthings.com/article/2009/03/002-surprised-by-calvin. Used with permission.

6. Saint Augustine, *Confessions and Enchiridion*, trans. Albert C. Outler (Grand Rapids: Christian Classics Ethereal Library, 2006), 2013. Available online at http://www.ccel.org/ccel/augustine/confessions.iv.html.

7. C. S. Lewis, *Letters to Malcolm: Chiefly on Prayer* (New York: Harcourt, 1964), 92.

ordinary experiences of pleasure and the kind of glory we will experience in heaven. And although they have cooled off quite a bit since then, Lewis observes, their basic disagreement has not been resolved. Lewis wants to insist that the mundane delight we take in things like dancing and playing games anticipates the kind of joy that awaits us in the afterlife, while Malcolm thinks that it is preposterous to compare such frivolous things to the glory we will experience in the heavenly realms.

Lewis holds firm. What Malcolm fails to understand, he says, is that even the most frivolous sorts of pleasures can function as "shafts of the [future] glory." Given the preoccupations of our present lives, says Lewis, we have a difficult time focusing directly on celestial matters. If we are to get any hint of what we will be experiencing in heaven, our only real opportunity is to catch a glimpse of the eternal "in activities which, for us here and now, are frivolous."[8]

Lewis's general thoughts on this subject are similar to those that Father Andrew Greeley sets forth in considerable detail in his book-length celebration of what he labels "the Catholic imagination." The things that make up our very ordinary existence, Greeley tells us, "hint at the nature of God," and they even serve to "make God in some fashion present to us."[9]

Of course, Lewis and Greeley make their cases in slightly different ways. For Lewis it is about how ordinary pleasurable experiences are anticipations of the future glory that God has promised for us. Greeley sees the ordinary things of life as providing us hints about the nature of God. They both are basically highlighting, however, different aspects of a shared view of reality, one that sees the visible world as pointing beyond itself to what is for us presently the realm of the invisible.

8. Lewis, *Letters to Malcolm*, 89.
9. Andrew Greeley, *The Catholic Imagination* (Berkeley: University of California Press, 2000), 6.

And this perspective in turn presents us with a particular view of the human person. In a very special way we humans point beyond ourselves. We are sacred icons who image something that transcends finite reality.

I have a confession to make: I like this way of viewing things. Indeed, I find it quite exciting. Now, this may not seem like a very dramatic confession to make on my part, so I have to add that I make this confession as a convinced Calvinist. And the fact is that both Lewis and Greeley go out of their way to single out Calvinism as a theological viewpoint that is especially hostile to the case they are each making. Greeley thinks that Calvinists are too negative about sex, for example. He describes the plot of a film, *Breaking the Waves*, where the heroine, Bess, lives in a somber Scottish Presbyterian community. Bess has a serious theological problem because she finds herself enjoying making love with her husband. Greeley tells us that she wants to express gratitude to God for the enjoyment of this pleasure, but she senses that the Lord is ready to receive her expressions of thanks for this only in "a grudging Calvinist way." Greeley is very sympathetic to Bess's plight and wishes that she had the opportunity to convert to Catholicism.[10]

Nor does Calvinism come off much better in Lewis's reflections on the ordinary pleasures. He reports to Malcolm that he had recently been reading Puritan writers, and he was reminded of how disagreeable he finds them. As a case in point he cites one Calvinist writer who says that in the deep places of his soul he sees nothing but "the Filth of a Dungeon."[11]

Now, it is important to note that Lewis was not meaning to suggest that everything is simply rosy in our inner lives.

10. Greeley, *Catholic Imagination*, 163.
11. Lewis, *Letters to Malcolm*, 98.

He admits that when he is looking into his own inner regions he sometimes sees some pretty bad stuff. The problem he has with the Puritan writers he has been reading is not that they discover sin in their private fantasies. The problem is that they turn what ought to be a periodic acknowledgment that our lives of pleasure are touched by sin into a way of life built on an ongoing disgust at the quite ordinary things that give us satisfaction.

I have to concede to both Greeley and Lewis that we Calvinists often have been overly negative in the ways they describe. We have felt obliged to go out of our way in emphasizing that we sinful humans have messed up badly, even in pursuing the very ordinary pleasures. Because we are so convinced of the all-pervasive character of human sinfulness, we have made it one of our special Calvinist callings to keep reminding other Christians that there is no dimension of our created life that does not afford a real—and often deceptively subtle—opportunity for rebelling against the will of God. In particular, then, while we have no problem admitting that the erotic aspect of our lives was a part of the creation that God originally called good, we also want to point to the real danger that under sinful conditions the erotic can become a staging area for a violation of the Creator's purposes. Our sexuality is one of the many aspects of fallen nature that needs to be redeemed.

So, while saying that I like the views that Greeley and Lewis set forth, I do want to issue the standard Calvinist warning about not offering any carte blanche endorsement of our natural yearnings and pleasures. For Christians, the term "natural" will always require some unpacking before we can engage in any discussion of human realities. "Natural" can refer to our *created* nature. In this sense it is perfectly legitimate to say that we humans are by nature good. But we can also use "natural" to refer to our *fallen* condition, and in that sense it is also important to say that we are by nature sinful.

Having paid my Calvinist dues, then, I can now explain why I like the way Greeley and Lewis encourage us to see human nature, even in its fallenness, as pointing beyond itself to a more ultimate reality. And this emphasis on the pointing beyond is what is so important about the notion, set forth in the very first chapter of the Bible, that human beings are created in the image and likeness of God. Human nature—certainly in its original unfallen manifestation—is, we can say, *iconic*. In our humanness we point beyond ourselves. As bearers of the image of God we reveal something about the nature of God. Nor has this iconic character been totally destroyed by our sinful rebellion. This is the central truth that has been embodied in the teaching—certainly the majority view in the Christian theological tradition—that the image of God in human beings, while it certainly has been distorted by sin, has nonetheless not been completely obliterated.

| Valued in Our Brokenness[12]

There is a nice story I once heard a priest tell about Pope John XXIII when he was still an Italian cardinal. He was having dinner one night with a priestly assistant who was reporting to the cardinal about another priest, a real renegade, who was doing things that were embarrassing the hierarchy. The future pope listened calmly, sipping wine from a goblet. Finally the assistant cried out in a frustrated tone, "How can you take this so calmly? Don't you realize what this priest is doing?" The cardinal then gently asked the younger priest, "Father, whose

12. Parts of this section are adapted from Mouw, "Elected for a Global Mission," 22–23, and Mouw, "Surprised by Calvin." Used with permission.

goblet is this?" "It is yours, your grace," the priest answered. The cardinal then threw the goblet to the floor, and it shattered into many fragments. "And now whose goblet is it?" he asked. "It is still yours," was the answer. "And so is this priest still my brother in Christ," said the cardinal, "even though he is shattered and broken."

The creation may be shattered and broken under present sinful conditions, but God still loves it. This is why Jesus came into the creation, on a redemptive mission aimed at restoring that which God loves. In Ephesians 4 the apostle Paul makes it clear that we cannot properly understand Christ's ascension into heaven until we have first grasped the fact that "he had also descended into the lower parts of the earth . . . so that he might fill all things" (Eph. 4:9–10 NRSV). And the love of Jesus goes so deep that he still suffers in and over the brokenness of the cosmos.

So what about those ordinary pleasures and desires? I get a lot of my theological insights from many of the older hymns, and I find Christmas carols to be an especially rich source of solid theology. One of my favorite lines is from "O Little Town of Bethlehem": "The hopes and fears of all the years are met in Thee tonight." The basic hopes and fears of the human heart, even the sinful human heart, are in some way fulfilled in the redemptive ministry of Jesus Christ.

To be sure, the yearnings of the sinful human heart are often fundamentally misdirected. I have been greatly helped in understanding how this goes from the writings of my friend James K. A. Smith.[13] When, because of our sinful rebellion, we cut ourselves off from a vital relationship with our Creator, we seek to satisfy our hopes and calm our fears by putting our ultimate

13. See especially, James K. A. Smith, *You Are What You Love: The Spiritual Power of Habit* (Grand Rapids: Brazos, 2016).

trust in something creaturely, in something that is less than the true God. But it is precisely because we are created for fellowship with the living God that the idols that we choose to serve never really satisfy our deepest yearnings.

And that is what is so helpful about the way Lewis makes his case to Malcolm. He insists that our longing for things eternal has very real connections to other kinds of longings. Even our most mundane quests for fulfillment, he argues, are in some important sense anticipations of the more lasting search for the kind of joy for which we have been created.

There is an illustration that is regularly attributed to G. K. Chesterton that gets at this point in a provocative manner. It goes like this: the man who knocks on the door of a house of prostitution is looking for God. I discovered recently that no one has been able to find that comment in Chesterton's writings, but that it does show up in a piece by a lesser known author.[14] Wherever the illustration actually comes from, it is provocative in a helpful way. Actually, when I first came across it, I was taken aback. The more I thought about it, though, the more I came to see it as making a profound point. Obviously the statement should not be taken as meaning that the man who approaches the house of prostitution hopes that God will be the one who greets him at the door. The real message is that people who are looking for ultimate fulfillment in the quest for sexual pleasure or wealth or power or any other element or aspect of creation will not find it in any of these things.

The Westminster Shorter Catechism makes the point clearly: our chief end as human beings is to glorify God and to enjoy *him* forever. Nothing brings ultimate fulfillment to the human spirit except an obedient relationship with our Creator.

14. Paul Nowak, "The Seven Most Popular G. K. Chesterton Quotes He Never Said," *The Federalist*, May 6, 2014, http://thefederalist.com/2014/05/06/the-seven -most-popular-g-k-chesterton-quotes-he-never-said/.

| Ultimate Fulfillment

I want to highlight the fact that what I have just been saying is our *ultimate* fulfillment. There are many things in life that fulfill us in good ways: eating a good meal, watching an entertaining movie, attending an exciting sports event. And, of course, the things that are more enduring: friendship, marriage, parent-child relationships.

I'll put the point bluntly here and then be careful to explain it. It isn't *all* about a relationship with God. In the marriage ceremony, for example, two Christians make a vow to God that they will love each other in both the joys and sorrows of life. Suppose, then, having made that vow, every time I do something as an act of faithfulness to that vow I think primarily of doing something that enhances my relationship with God. My wife says to me, "Thanks for cooking that meal this evening. It was good." Then I say, "I did it for the Lord." When I give her a gift for her birthday I make sure she knows that I was doing it out of a desire to be faithful to God. And so on.

Surely at some point she would have a perfect right to respond: "What about *me*? Don't you get satisfaction out of doing things that make *me* happy? Don't you give gifts to *me*? What about *our* companionship?"

I have no question that God would endorse her complaints. In Psalm 104:31, the psalmist proclaims, "May the LORD rejoice in his works." Only after many verses echoing God's satisfaction with his creation do humans make their first appearance. The Lord clearly wants us to take delight in what he has created. This includes also what he has included in his creating purposes, in which we humans can experience flourishing. In our efforts to glorify God and enjoy him forever, then, it is important that we attend to all that brings glory to God.

The Lord fashioned human beings in a way that we would not only take good care of the nonhuman creation but flourish in friendships and families, as well as in producing and enjoying good art, and in making use of the other gifts and talents that he provided for in creating us as individuals.

What I need to be and do as a husband and father, then, is to honor God's creating and redeeming purposes for marriage and family. Given those purposes, it would be a bad thing for me to give my wife and son the impression that whatever good I might do in my relationship with them I am really doing it "for the Lord." There are times, of course, when we do need to remind ourselves that the Lord wants us to be faithful to his purposes in our relationships. But being faithful in these matters does mean that we take those relationships themselves—with those very real individual human beings—with utmost seriousness.

So again: our *ultimate* satisfaction is to be found in God alone. But that does not mean ignoring the other satisfactions in life. To glorify God in these matters is to see the range of human relationships and activities within a perspective that takes with ultimate seriousness the will of the Creator.

Ultimate Trust

What does this way of viewing things say about people who have not put their ultimate trust in the God of the Bible? The obvious answer is that it is idolatry to put our ultimate trust in anything but God. And I accept that answer. It is important, though, not simply to stop there.

The apostle Paul did not just stop there with the Athenians in the encounter reported in Acts 17. He was asked to talk about his own faith perspective in a setting surrounded by idols to many gods, including one to "an unknown god." He knew idolatry when he saw it. "He was greatly distressed to see that the city was full of idols" (Acts 17:16).

But when Paul began to speak to the Athenians he did not begin with a condemnation of idolatry. Instead he commented about the religious longings that were on display. "People of Athens! I see that in every way you are very religious" (17:22). Then he made this intriguing comment with reference to the "unknown god" altar: "You are ignorant of the very thing you worship—and this is what I am going to proclaim to you" (17:23). He was probing more deeply into their idolatrous patterns.

While on an extended visit to a college community, my wife and I once socialized on several occasions with a married couple with three young children. We not only enjoyed being with these folks, but we also admired the commitment of the parents to their children. The couple professed no interest in religion, but it was clear that the things they cared about deeply were of the kind that we would hope for in a Christian family. When we mentioned to them once how much we admired their devotion, the wife responded, "Family is everything to us."

We lost touch with these folks for several years. Then I met the husband at an academic gathering. "There has been a big change in our lives," he said. "My wife and I have accepted Christ. We came to realize that there was something seriously missing in our lives. Now we are a Christian family!"

It was clear from his conversation at that point that they still greatly valued their family life. But the commitment to family was no longer ultimate for them. They were now engaging in all of the things they had previously valued in ways that were directed to the glory of God.

Suppose I had tried to witness about the gospel to them when we had first met them and simply told them that they were idolaters. In a basic theological sense I would have been correct. But it would not have communicated the real good news.

Their deep commitment to family was a good thing. It was not ultimately satisfying for them, however. "We came to realize that there was something seriously missing in our lives." They could now, as believers, devote their family life—reordering it where necessary in the light of revelation—to the glory of God.

| Standing Alongside

As a seminary student I took a course titled "Theology of Religion," focusing on different theological understandings from a Christian perspective on non-Christian religions. The professor had us read three books. One propounded the view that the diverse religions were all paths to the same goal. The second one saw the truth of God in Christ as a judgment on all religions.

The third book gave the perspective with which our professor agreed—and it worked with me. The author, Stephen Neill, who was a bishop of the Church of South India, was committed to the affirmation that Jesus Christ is the one true Savior. But unlike the author of the second book, he encouraged a posture of standing alongside persons of other faiths, taking seriously the concerns that they raise about the basic issues of life. I found his comments about Hinduism especially helpful. We must approach the Hindu "from within Hinduism," he wrote, "putting questions to the Hindu and helping the Hindu understand himself better." In doing this, he explained, "the Christian will be attempting to help the Hindu to see the radical unsatisfactoriness of all the answers that have been given to his questions and so to point him to the one in whom those questions can receive their all-sufficient answer, the Lord Jesus Christ."[15]

15. Stephen Neill, *Christian Faith and Other Faiths* (Downers Grove, IL: InterVarsity, 1984), 98.

That approach came to characterize my approach to non-Christian thought and life in general. We stand alongside people, listening to them, attempting to discern their deepest hopes and fears. We ask questions, probing for the underlying spiritual dynamics—the Augustinian restlessness at work in their deep places. And we look for opportunities to point to the One in whom restless hearts can find true satisfaction.

| Real Evil

I was setting forth that way of viewing things in a talk I gave about civility, and in the question-and-answer period someone posed a blunt challenge to me: "So if you had a chance to talk to Hitler would you engage in dialogue with him, standing alongside him to probe his deepest hopes and fears?"

I did not need to hesitate in giving a straightforward response. I would not dialogue with Hitler. If I got near him at all it would be with the intention of putting an end to his wicked deeds, using whatever means available to me. (I am not a pacifist.)

Here, though, is a different scenario. Suppose I had a chance these days to talk to a teenager—a member of a skinhead group—who professes to be firmly convinced of a neo-Nazi ideology. Let's say, furthermore, that the young man's concerned parents asked me to talk to him about his philosophical views, and their son agreed to talk.

In this case I *would* talk about hopes and fears. The Nazi ideology is based on a desire to form and preserve "a master race" purged of "impure" elements. In what I take to be a profound sense, this perspective is a horribly perverse version of what the apostle Peter tells us about our redeemed identities: "You are a chosen race, a royal priesthood, a holy nation, God's own people" (1 Pet. 2:9 NRSV).

In my teens I heard a right-wing fundamentalist preacher denouncing "unity" schemes. The devil, he said, is trying to create one world race, one world church, and one world government. We true Christians, the preacher urged, have to thwart Satan's designs by opposing the civil rights efforts, the ecumenical movement, and the United Nations. This did not sound right to me at the time, but it was only later that I realized 1 Peter 2:9 addresses that very agenda. Jesus came to establish new unities—a new kind of "chosen race," a new kind of "royal priesthood," and a new kind of "God's own people."

The problem in our present world is that there are indeed Satan-inspired counterfeit "unities." I don't identify the same ones that the fundamentalist preacher did, but we do need to be on guard against being lured into false promises of oneness.

The neo-Nazis have come to believe the lie about one of those counterfeits—a new kind of racial "purity." That is based on a horrible satanic lie. The unity that Christ brings through the power of the Spirit draws together members from different tribes, tongues, peoples, and nations into a new community made possible through the blood that was shed on Calvary. To yearn for any other kind of unity is to misdirect our longings and loves.

| 8 |

About Quoting Hymns

Someone asked me if I was working on another book, and I told them about this one. "I hope you write about why you like hymns so much!" the person said.

Actually, I had been thinking about devoting a chapter here to hymns. But it's not really about my "like" for hymns. That would not justify my including a discussion here. I want to say some things about how the *use* of hymns can build us up for communal faithfulness. Musical expressions in general, and hymns in particular, have the power to reach into our souls in a special way.

But there is a larger point I want to make. We need to find ways to be reached deeply in our souls. I'll get to that after some thoughts about the spiritual power of hymnody.

| Attending to Implications

I was speaking to a church group on a Saturday afternoon—it was a retreat setting—and most of the people attending were either close to retirement or already there. The subject of worship came up, and one man asked me, with a tone of irritation, "What can we do about all this 'contemporary music' stuff? I find it repetitious and loud. Why do the young folks in our church like it so much?"

I was tempted to be a bit harsh in my response. There is something a little strange about asking a guest speaker who is visiting the questioner's church for the first time about the music preferences of young people in that church. On that question I was the least likely person in the room to have an answer.

In my answer, though, I decided to address what I saw as the heart of his concern. He was genuinely disturbed by generational differences in preferences regarding the proper music in worship. I proposed that it might be a good idea for the folks in that room to invite some of the younger members for a conversation about that subject. And rather than employing a confrontational tone, they could ask the young folks what they hoped for when they came to church to worship. What kind of music serves for them to express praise to God? And, I said, the older folks could answer the same question. I urged them to frame the conversation in a way that members from both generations could actually come to understand each other better.

I understood the frustrations that informed the man's question to me. I have heard those frustrations expressed by many folks of my generation. I don't experience those frustrations to the same degree. I want to get around to explaining why in this chapter. But first I need to explain my own fondness for the more traditional hymns and the use to which I put them.

When I have quoted from a hymn, I have typically meant to be drawing out the implications of expressions in the hymn with which my audience is familiar. That made good sense as long as the people whom I was addressing were familiar with the hymns I was quoting. Musical preferences in worship have changed significantly in recent decades, so I have had to change my habits. While I still make considerable use of the older hymns in my personal devotional life, I can't assume that other evangelicals know the words.

Drawing out the implications of familiar hymns is something I did a lot when some of us were promoting a new "evangelical social action" in the 1970s. For example, when Ron Sider and I once spoke to an evangelical audience about "the gospel and the poor," one of our listeners was agitated. He said that Sider's views about programs for serving the poor were "not from the Bible—it is straight out of Karl Marx."

I came to Sider's defense by appealing to the authority of George Beverly Shea, the longtime soloist at Billy Graham's crusades. I recounted the time in my childhood when our family bought our first record player. One of the first records we owned was Shea singing hymns. I played that record over and over again, more out of fascination with the new technology than with any deep spiritual impulse. But I did manage to memorize all the hymns on the record.

I told the audience that listening to Shea was my first lesson in economics. Then I quoted one of the soloist's favorites: "I'd rather have Jesus than silver or gold, / I'd rather be His than have riches untold / I'd rather have Jesus than houses or land, / I'd rather be led by His nail-pierced hand." Once you've learned that kind of thing from George Beverly Shea, I said, Karl Marx's economics can seem rather tame!

Well, maybe I overdid that a little bit, but the basic point still strikes me as a good one. If one has been inspired by what were then very familiar words in evangelicalism, the question of what we do with our money is, in a basic sense, settled. We must use our worldly goods to follow Jesus. And then the only important questions are: Does Jesus care about the poor? And if he does, how should we be faithful in representing that concern in our own lives? Needless to say, there is much to argue about in terms of governmental programs, Christian charity, and the like. But those of us who have testified that we would "rather have Jesus than silver or gold" cannot avoid the challenges.

| Reinforcing

In large part, my use of hymns in my writing and speaking has been for their—and I know that I am risking a bad pun here—instrumental value. They are one of the items that we as speakers can draw up from our rhetorical repertoire in our efforts to convince an audience of something that we want to get across.

Here is an example of my instrumental use of a line from a hymn. A pastor asked me to speak at a weeknight event in his congregation about issues surrounding race relations. This area of concern had become quite controversial in their local community, and people in his congregation were divided about whether they as Christians should be addressing the topics.

I agreed to the assignment and prepared some careful comments on the relationship of biblical teaching to questions of racial justice. The evening began with a dinner in the church hall, and then we went into the sanctuary, where we had a time of worship before my talk. We began by singing "O Worship the King." Just before I spoke, the all-white children's choir sang "Jesus loves the little children, / all the children of the world; / red and yellow, black and white, / they are precious in his sight."

I started my talk by discussing the singing that had already taken place that evening. We started off, I said, addressing God as "King." Then the children gave us a very powerful message: the King loves black kids, as well as those who are red and yellow and white. What more do we need to say by way of establishing that the Christian gospel addresses issues of race relationships? The basic premise has been established, and having established the Savior's love for children of different races, what remains are the practical questions: What are we going to do about that as his followers? How can we not think about the quality of education in our schools, and about the prejudices that continue to influence the patterns of public life?

What I did in that case was to pay attention to the actual commitments that people had made in the words they had sung. This kind of thing takes no special skill on my part. It simply requires paying close attention to what is going on in our musical poetry, and encouraging people to take seriously what they have already affirmed in their singing.

| Providing Wisdom

There is a second use of hymnody, though, that has also been important to me. This usage requires staying alert to theological clues that hymns make available to us. In this case, then, the hymn actually becomes an important theological resource. It does not just give us a way to reinforce what we already know theologically—the instrumental use—but it actually *contributes to* our theological knowledge.

My most recent case in point of learning theology from a hymn comes from "Crown Him with Many Crowns." I have sung it many times over the years; I can go through the four standard verses without having to glance at the words. Recently, though, these particular words leapt out at me in a worship service:

> Crown him the Lord of love;
> Behold his hands and side,
> Rich wounds, yet visible above,

In beauty glorified:
No angel in the sky
Can fully bear that sight,
But downward bends his burning eye
At mysteries so bright.

That the wounds of Jesus are "yet visible above" is not a surprising thought. When Jesus appears as the one who alone is worthy to open the scroll in Revelation 5, John reports that he saw "a Lamb, looking as if it had been slain" (Rev. 5:6). There is nothing jarring about the idea that when the risen Savior ascended into the heavens he did so with nail-pierced hands.

The phrase that I found theologically jarring, though, was that the wounds of Jesus are now "in beauty glorified." In the heavenly context, those wounds have taken on a glorious beauty. And their splendor is such that the angels cannot gaze on them. Yet—and this is an amazing thing—we as redeemed human beings are called to "behold his hands and side."

As soon as I began to think about this profound verse, my mind went to some lines from another old hymn—one that was popular in my childhood, but which I have not heard for years.

Holy, Holy, is what the angels sing;
And I expect to help them make the courts of heaven
ring.
But when I sing redemption's story, they will fold their
wings.
For angels never felt the joy that our salvation brings.

The theological suggestion here seems right to me. We redeemed humans can grasp the significance of the person and work of Christ in a way that the angels cannot. They have not experienced the actually transforming work of the incarnation, cross, and resurrection.

The "rich wounds" lines take this point further, however. It is crucial to our eternal destinies that we actually "behold" the glorification of the wounds of Jesus. We will behold the beauty of the nail prints in a way that angels cannot grasp.

In recent years the theology of disabilities has become a specific topic in theological discussion. Not that the questions have been completely ignored in the past, but they have now come to constitute an identifiable area of scholarly exploration. And while there are significant issues having to do with our understanding of serving the disabled in church and society, the eschatological issues—topics pertaining to the afterlife—are also of great interest. I am far from an expert in the field, but I do find the issues important and fascinating. The following example is a good case in point.

Molly was a woman with Down syndrome who died at age thirty. Her family provided her with the best educational and occupational resources available, and she was able to learn to read books for children on a third-grade level. Molly loved to sing and early memorized the songs that she sang as a member of a church choir. Molly especially loved to sing "Jesus Loves Me," and it was clear to all that her enthusiasm for the song was an expression of her deep love for the Savior.

Molly's family members know that she is with Jesus in heaven now, and they look forward to seeing her when they too pass on from this life. What will they encounter when they are reunited with Molly, though? In one important sense, Molly's having Down syndrome was very much a part of who she was on her earthly pilgrimage, and it is hard to imagine that in her transformed heavenly condition she will be completely unrecognizable in this regard.

Here is what I think it is reasonable to believe. Molly's Down syndrome-ness will be "in beauty glorified," much like the wounds of Jesus. It is not altogether misleading to refer to

Down syndrome—as I have been doing here—as a disability. But persons with Down syndrome are also "abled" in special ways. Molly's family will tell you that she brought distinct gifts into their lives. In a profound sense, they testify, she *ministered* to them in incomparable ways. All of this will be marvelously enhanced in heaven—"in beauty glorified."

| Poetic Memories

David Hubbard put it well once in a conversation. Hymns, he said, are "the collective theological memories of the church in poetic form." I have already pointed to the theological importance of memory. But the "poetic" part of what Hubbard said also needs to be emphasized.

I was fascinated to read a lengthy feature in the *New Yorker* magazine about Daniel Dennett, a scholar well known for his vocal rejection of religious belief. He and his wife are disdainful of Christian convictions, yet each year they invite friends to their home for an evening of carol singing. They profess to love—and even to be inspired by—the songs proclaiming the birth of Christ.

That does not surprise me. Poetic expression has many uses, but one obvious feature is its power to inspire. It reaches deeper than our intellect. And musical poetry in particular has the capacity to reach deep into our souls, stirring up emotions that are not completely controlled by cognition.

This is certainly true for more than religious music. I experienced the power of patriotic music a few days after the horrible destruction of 9/11. As a product of the 1960s, having participated in many antiwar protests, I spent several decades pretty much unaffected by displays of patriotism. Not that I have ever been anti-American. I typically held my hand over my heart at events when the national anthem was sung, and I have never refrained from saying the Pledge of Allegiance to the flag. But I typically experienced some emotional distance from those rituals.

On a weekend evening after the horrific events in New York City, we went to the Hollywood Bowl for a concert. The program always begins, as darkness settles in, with a spotlight on the American flag while the national anthem is played. I surprised myself by beginning to sob as the anthem was played. The ritual connected to me in a deep place. I *felt* patriotic. The anthem stirred up something in me—feelings that had long been latent.

In my Calvinist world we have made much of buried *thoughts* in the life of the unbeliever. And there is a good biblical basis for emphasizing the cognitive in this regard. The apostle Paul puts the point bluntly in Romans 1:18. In a sense, he says, people who are living lives of rebellion against God really do know better. But they "suppress the truth by their wickedness."

But the rebellion goes deeper than just the cognitive. And when the gift of regeneration enables us to express more truthful thoughts, that to which we give our cognitive assent is undergirded by gratitude and wonder. While I subscribe, for example, to the *doctrine* of the substitutionary atoning work of Christ, it takes on new dimensions for me when I sing Charles Wesley's "And Can It Be?": "Amazing love, how can it be / that Thou my God shouldst die for me?"

| Sentimentalism[1]

I do know, of course, that making too much of the deeper-than-cognitive reach of hymns can be used to justify the superficiality

---

1. Parts of this section are adapted from Richard J. Mouw, "Alone in the Garden?," *First Things*, July 1, 2016, https://www.firstthings.com/blogs/first thoughts/2016/07/alone-in-the-garden. Used with permission.

of sentimentalism. And much of what many of us older folks often have in mind by "the great hymns of the past" provides strong doses of sentimentality. Sometimes those celebrations of "wonderful peace" and "joy in my heart" need to be set aside as we sing songs of genuine lament. But we scholarly types also need to be sure that we are being fair when we deny the legitimacy of what we might quickly label as an overly "sentimental" musical expression.

The historian Mark Noll and I once coedited a volume of essays—papers that had been given at a Wheaton College conference—on evangelical hymns. Noll is the real expert on the subject. I know a lot about evangelical hymns primarily because I sang so many of them in my early years, and many of the lines have stuck with me.

In the course of putting that book of readings together, Noll and I had some stimulating discussions about hymns, and I learned much from him on the subject. On one particular hymn, though, I resisted his criticism. "In the Garden" was highly popular with previous generations of evangelicals, and it uses much popular "love song" imagery: "He speaks, and the sound of his voice is so sweet / that the birds hush their singing" and "He walks with me / and he talks with me, / and he tells me I am his own."

Noll objected to this imagery—and truth be told, I knew he was right. I really had to resort to much attempted cleverness to defend this line in particular: "And the joy we share as we tarry there, / none other has ever known." That really is too much. Can I really sing about a relationship with the Lord that is so joyous that no other person has ever experienced it? Doesn't this go beyond the bounds of hyperbolic spiritual enthusiasm?

Okay, Noll had that right. What kept me at it in the discussion, though, was that my reluctance to condemn the song is based on family bonds. The song was a favorite of my parents, and each of them requested that it be sung at their funerals. On those two occasions I sang it with much feeling. I won't go into the lengths I went to in my resistance to Noll's wisdom. Suffice it to say, I finally gave it up as a lost cause—while still wanting to honor my parents' affection for the song.

Then, however, Noll reopened the discussion in a way that we both considered a fitting conclusion to our previous exchanges. He showed me a published testimony of a mainland Chinese pastor who had been placed in a detention camp during the Cultural Revolution. Each day he was lowered into a pit filled with human feces and ordered to start shoveling. He was able to endure this horrific indignity, he reported, by singing over and over again the words to "In the Garden." He was refusing, he said, to allow his captors to define his reality for him. He chose to see himself as enjoying the presence of his Savior.

Noll found that testimony quite moving. "I can see now that a lot depends on the context," he said to me. I agreed. And while that one line about "none other has ever known" is still, even in that detention camp context, at best a bit of hyperbole, in the Chinese pastor's case a little hyperbole served a cause that went well beyond a mere spiritual sentimentalism.

What that example shows is the capacity that hymns have for undergirding and reinforcing our worldviewing. And whether we stick with more traditional hymnody or come up with new musical expressions, that larger purpose is crucial to our sense of who we are as followers of Christ.

| Throne Room Worship

None of what I have been saying here is intended as a case for simply returning to the hymnody of the past. I do hope that the best of those hymns are not forever lost to evangelicalism, but much of what I enjoyed singing in the past can be left in the past.

Actually, I am convinced that much of the recent praise music in evangelicalism is good for the worshiping life of the church. One of the most important liturgical developments in recent decades in the evangelical world has been the introduction of the screen in worship, and its presence in our sanctuaries has transformed our worshiping patterns in positive ways. Looking down at the pages of a hymnbook that we are holding in our hands is no longer the typical singing posture in many churches. This means that we are free to use our bodies in different ways in worship. We can raise our hands in praise if we are so inclined. And even if we are too stodgy to do that, our eyes are directed upward rather than downward.

The content of much contemporary worship music is also quite solid. "In Christ Alone" and "How Deep the Father's Love for Us" are obvious examples of hymns that are theologically and spiritually rich. But many of the other simpler songs focus on the divine majesty, which is essential to proper worship. When we gather for Christian worship we are entering the divine throne room, wherein it is important to be made aware that—in the words of Jack Hayford's "Majesty"—God's "kingdom authority flow from his throne unto his own."

I should add that I have difficulty taking the complaints about "repetitious praise songs" seriously. I was raised on much more superficial evangelical repetition: "Do Lord, oh do Lord, oh do remember me / Do Lord, oh do Lord, oh do remember me . . ." and "I have the joy, joy, joy, joy down in my heart, down in my heart, down in my heart."

Those songs were superficial in their repetitiveness. But repeating more profound words can be an effective element in spiritual formation. During the same period in which much of our contemporary worship has been developed, we evangelicals have also been emphasizing the importance of the practices of spirituality. Some of the best lessons we have learned have come from the monastic tradition. And monks repeat themselves a lot: "Kyrie, Kyrie, Kyrie." Those words, put to music, are worth repeating!

| 9 |

Embracing Mystery

When Rob Bell's book *Love Wins* appeared in 2011, it stirred up quite a bit of controversy. One prominent evangelical theologian immediately voted Rob off the evangelical island with a three-word tweet: "Farewell Rob Bell." When a reporter from *USA Today* called to ask me for my assessment, I told her that I thought it was a good book that raised some important questions, and that for each seemingly controversial issue that Rob raised, you could find some solidly orthodox theologian in the past exploring similar territory—the early church theologian Irenaeus is an obvious case in point as is, more recently, C. S. Lewis. What made Rob's book particularly bracing, then, was the provocative *manner* in which he touched on these edgier topics.

In offering a favorable comment about his book, I did not take as much flak as Rob did for actually writing it. I did get some negative criticisms, however, for my refusal to join Rob's harsher critics. But I also heard from many folks who thanked me for defending *Love Wins*. The testimony of one woman particularly pleased me. She had been an evangelical Calvinist for all of her seventy-plus years, she said, but in the past decade or so she had been privately entertaining the very questions that Rob addressed. She was not completely comfortable with his answers to those questions, but she was grateful that he provided some guidance for her own spiritual quest. And she thanked me for saying that it is good to wrestle with these questions without being able to come up with quick answers. "Like you," she said, "I have been learning to make room for some mystery when I think theologically about these things."

| Mystery for Evangelicals

The woman who thanked me for saying something good about Bell's book put it well when she said that "when I think *theologically* about these things" she was making room for mystery. We evangelicals are no strangers to mystery, but we tend to keep it contained within our spiritual expressions. We often get quite nervous when it spills over too much into our theology.

I draw much strength from the way that mystery looms so large in our evangelical spirituality. We sing fervently about God's "matchless grace." We "scarce can take it in" when we think about how God did not spare his only Son in saving us. And Charles Wesley spoke of "Amazing love, how can it be / that Thou my God shouldst die for me?"

Those lines, of course, come from those older hymns that don't get sung as much these days in evangelical worship. But newer musical expressions are no less focused on mystery. Consider these lyrics from "How Deep the Father's Love for Us" by Stuart Townend:

> How deep the Father's love for us,
> How vast beyond all measure,
> That He should give His only Son
> To make a wretch His treasure.

Also noteworthy are these words from "Shout to the Lord" by
Darlene Zschech:

> My Jesus, my Savior,
> Lord, there is none like You.
> All of my days, I want to praise
> The wonders of Your mighty love.

Essential to an evangelical expression of faith in God is a
strong sense of wonder and awe in the presence of the creating
and redeeming power of the Almighty. And the clear implica-
tion of these spiritual expressions is that our words, our efforts
to capture these realities in theological formulations, will inevitably fail to capture adequately our sense of wonder and awe.

Again, though, when we formulate all of this theologically,
we evangelicals typically become quite precise. Our liberal arts
colleges and universities require faculty members—whatever
their field of specialty—to sign statements of faith that are
often quite detailed. The seminary versions of these statements
are even more detailed. And candidates for ordination in our
churches are often required to submit to rigorous doctrinal
examinations. More than any other branch of Christianity, we
still conduct our own versions of heresy trials.

What is going on in this? Why the pairing of spiritual wonder
at the mysteries of God's creating and redeeming purposes with
an insistence on fairly precise theological formulation?

Let me say up front that I endorse the practices associated
with careful theological monitoring. I have lived with those
practices happily throughout my academic career. I have often
remarked that the difference between the theological expecta-
tions during my seventeen years on the Calvin College faculty
and my subsequent decades at Fuller Theological Seminary
comes down to about ninety-nine pages of theology. When I

joined the Calvin faculty I had to subscribe to, in addition to the early ecumenical creeds (Apostles', Nicene), the confessional documents of the Dutch Reformed tradition: the Heidelberg Catechism, the Belgic Confession, and the Canons of the Synod of Dort—totaling about a hundred pages of theological subject matter. I signed my name on the Calvinist dotted line with genuine affirmation.

Fuller Seminary, however, has a one-page, ten-point statement of faith, a consensus document that faculty from a variety of perspectives—Wesleyan, Reformed, Baptist, Pentecostal, Anglican, Lutheran, "none of the above" new-style ecclesial congregations—all affirm. And a candidate for a faculty position who has made it to the final stage of consideration must write eight to ten pages explaining his or her understanding of the contents of that statement, a paper that then becomes the basis for an hour-and-a-half oral "theology exam" conducted by the tenured faculty. The Fuller statement may be only a page in length, but the discussion of its content with a faculty candidate regularly gets into fine detail. And there have been instances where a candidate is not found to be theologically acceptable.

I care deeply about the fine details. So what does that have to do with my eagerness, as the woman who contacted me put it, "to make room for some mystery when I think *theologically* about these things"?

Here is where I find it necessary to make a distinction between what I experience spiritually and what I try to formulate theologically. The distinction I have in mind is helped along for me by the way the Catholic theologian Thomas Weinandy describes the nature of the theological task. Theology, he says, is not so much "a problem solving" exercise as it is "a mystery discerning enterprise." To solve a problem is not to make all of our puzzles go away. Puzzle solving is not the kind of resolution that we ought to expect as a matter of course in theological exploration. What we can hope for, Weinandy says, is to ascertain "more precisely and clearly what the mystery is"—and this can be an important gain.[1]

The relationship Weinandy is pointing to seems to be exactly right. There is much mystery that we need to allow for in theology. But at the same time it is not an anything-goes enterprise. We also need to work at knowing some things "precisely and clearly" about that which is surrounded by mystery.

Here is where I do have to express some worry about how Bell makes his case in *Love Wins*. He says there that he is not sure that Gandhi ended up in hell. This has disturbed some evangelicals, but I do not find it upsetting. Can I be sure that God sent Gandhi to hell? No. The question of how God gets ahold of people and decides their destinies is something we can simply leave in God's hands.

But here are some things about that question that we *can* be precise and clear about: Jesus alone saves. We are not saved by our good works. Salvation is by grace alone. And the saving grace of God has been made possible for sinners like us only through the redemptive mission that culminated in the death and resurrection of the Son of God.

So let me be clear in saying this: if Gandhi *was* received into heaven when he died, it was only because of the blood that was shed on Calvary. Jesus Christ alone can save.

| The "Unsearchable"

There was a time when I was quite frustrated in my attempts to understand what the apostle Paul says in Romans 11 about God's continuing relationship to the Jewish people. Paul seems

---

1. Thomas G. Weinandy, *Does God Suffer?* (Notre Dame, IN: University of Notre Dame Press, 2000), 32–34.

to go back and forth: Israel's rejection of Jesus as the heaven-sent Messiah is seriously displeasing to God; they are branches that have been broken off and a wild shoot has been grafted in their place (11:17). But then Paul warns the gentile Christians that they should not take this as cause for pride, since the Jews are still the "natural branches" who will eventually be grafted back onto the tree (11:24). Does this mean, then, that Israel as a people will be saved? Well, "For God has bound everyone over to disobedience so that he may have mercy on them all" (11:32). Having read Paul thus far on the subject, I am eager to have him answer a few more important questions for clarification. But instead he just gives expression to a sense of profound mystery concerning the ways of God:

> Oh, the depth of the riches of the wisdom and knowl-
> edge of God!
> How unsearchable his judgments,
> and his paths beyond tracing out!
> "Who has known the mind of the Lord?
> Or who has been his counselor?"
> "Who has ever given to God,
> that God should repay them?"
> For from him and through him and for him are all
> things.
> To him be the glory forever! Amen.
>
> Romans 11:33–36

On the question concerning God's continuing purposes with the present-day ethnic descendants of the ancient Israelites, I have learned to join Paul in singing hymns to the mysteries of God's dealings with humankind. But I have also had to acknowledge that this has important implications for my theological formulations. Spiritual mystery entails a significant degree of theological mystery.

| Messiness?

I must make a confession here. In discussing the theological variety of mystery with my students I have sometimes used a less noble-sounding word, referring to my increasing sense of a need for some "messiness" in my theology. Actually, there is something I like about "messy" as it applies to theology. I would never, of course, use it to describe the spiritual side of things. I don't want a messy spirituality—"mystery" is the right word for encountering the wonders of what God has done for us in Christ. But when I work at thinking theologically about such things, "messy" seems quite appropriate at times.

Allowing for theological messiness serves a number of helpful functions in dealing with theological matters. For one thing, it keeps me aware of the tentativeness of much of what I am coming up with theologically. I once gave talks on a campus where my hosts had paired me with a speaker whose views were somewhat different from my own on some important topics. Each of us was assigned the same set of topics, and at each session we were to present our differing understandings of one of those topics.

For our first session the other speaker went first. Before presenting his prepared remarks, he said that he wanted to clarify something important at the outset. Someone had described this engagement, he said, as "a dialogue between Dr. Mouw and myself." He had no interest in dialogue, he said. "I am here to battle for the hearts and minds of people in this campus community!"

When it was my turn to speak, I began by saying that I did not see myself as an intellectual warrior. I promised to listen carefully to what the other speaker had to say, and if he convinced me that I was wrong about something, or that I had to seriously revise my views on some topic, I would do my best to respond in that way. "If I have to admit that I am wrong about what I said previously," I said, "no one here should feel betrayed."

That was not just a piece of rhetoric for me. I not only enjoy dialogue—I need it. Back-and-forth with others is the way I learn. I have changed my mind many times over the decades of my intellectual journey. I have learned to be comfortable with some intellectual—and more specifically, theological—messiness.

But I do know that "messy" can be dangerous as applied to theology. This is why I find it necessary always to keep it closely linked to a sense of mystery. I do that to avoid sloppy theology. The kind of messiness I value is not endorsing fuzzy ideas but, rather, embracing clear ideas that stand in some kind of tension with each other.

The theology of the Trinity is a good case in point for this. There are three persons of the Godhead, but they are not three distinct Gods. They are one God in three persons. To put it that way is to set forth solid orthodox theology. But it is also for me somewhat messy. If I make too much of the "one God" part of it, I start sounding like a modalist—the view that the three titles, Father, Son, and Spirit, are simply different titles for one person. But if I go the other way, emphasizing the three persons too much, I start sounding like a tri-theist, the view that there really are three different Gods.

So I hold on to two straightforward theological claims—one God, three persons—in a kind of tension, without knowing exactly how to formulate how they fit together in a fully coherent manner. I stand in awe of the mystery of the eternal Trinity while allowing for some messiness in how I articulate my theological understanding.

Most Christians would take a similar approach about the Trinity. And much the same can apply to other pairs of teachings that we hold in a kind of tension. Jesus of Nazareth was fully God and fully human. God exercises sovereign control over all things, and we humans are responsible for the choices we make.

There are some areas, though, where an openness to the messy can trigger some danger alarms, and I have done some of that triggering myself, particularly in an area already briefly touched upon: who is "in" and who is "out" in terms of salvation. The issues here are especially poignant these days with reference to non-Christian religions. I have been actively engaged in interfaith dialogue, and I want to focus on that topic in the next chapter.

| 10 |

Neighborly Dialogue

A local congregation invited me to do a weeknight talk at their church about the Mormon-evangelical dialogue that I have been codirecting since 2000. I said I would do it if local Mormons were also invited. They gladly complied, and the local Latter-day Saint (LDS) folks were pleased to be invited. They came in good numbers. We left plenty of time for a question-and-answer period, and there were some fine interactions.

Afterward there were refreshments—the evangelicals thoughtfully served no coffee on this occasion! Over lemonade and cookies, many friendly informal conversations took place. At one point, two couples who had been talking together motioned for me to join them. "Thank you for helping us to get to know our Mormon neighbors," the evangelical woman said. "We have lived next door to each other for ten years, and we have waved to each other often, but this is the first time we have actually talked. We just did not know how to break the ice in getting to know each other. But we just agreed to spend some time together!"

I have come to appreciate that "break the ice" factor. My own focus for several decades has been on the sort of interfaith encounters that take place among "elites"—religious leaders and academic types who specialize in the study of various religious perspectives. I enjoy that kind of encounter and recognize—and argue for—its importance.

The two couples who were getting to know each other as neighbors, however, were not likely skilled in that kind of dialogue. There is a likelihood that on many issues that are at stake in comparing Mormon thought with traditional Christian understandings of key matters, they are not all that secure in explaining the theological basis for their respective convictions, even to people who share those convictions.

One thing we could do to correct that, of course, is to provide more detailed theological education for our church members, so that when they talk to, say, Mormon neighbors they will provide careful accounts of the doctrine of the Trinity, the two natures of Christ, the nature of biblical authority, and the like.

I am not convinced, however, that every sincere believer should feel obligated to be so articulate in such theological matters in conversations with persons of other faiths. In any event, that is not what the couple who had just met their Mormon neighbors were referring to in their "break the ice" comment. They had felt awkward about simply getting a conversation going with their Mormon neighbors. Suppose, for example, they happened to be at their mailboxes at the same time, and it was clear that this was a time to introduce themselves. And suppose the Mormon woman mentioned that she and her husband had just returned from a conference in Salt Lake City, with the explanation that "We are members of the LDS." What does an evangelical Christian say? "Oh, that's nice"? Or, "Well, we are Bible-believing Christians"? And where might the conversation go from there?

Here is a real-life example. An evangelical business leader called me to ask about evangelicals and Mormons. "I know about your Mormon-evangelical dialogue," he said, "and I need some practical advice." One of his business partners was LDS, and they often had lunch together to talk about work issues. "He knows I am an evangelical," the caller said, "and the other day he said he would like to pray before our meal. His prayer was one that I could have offered up. So here is my question: The next time we eat together, should I offer to pray? Or is doing that some sort of compromise with unbelief?"

I encouraged him to pray with his colleague, and—if appropriate—to ask him about the role of prayer in his life. And he should not be afraid to talk about Jesus. Nor should he feel that he has to win a theological argument in doing so. Simply showing a genuine interest about how his LDS friend understands what it means to have a relationship with Jesus is a good thing.

I also told him about a good book to read, if he were so inclined: Terry Muck's *Those Other Religions in Your Neighborhood: Loving Your Neighbor When You Don't Know How*.[1] The very title of that book tells the story. One does not have to be a gifted theologian to have a loving relationship with someone of another faith. It is just a matter of learning to be a good neighbor. A key trait in this regard is a kind of spiritual *empathy*—genuinely wanting to know more about the person in one's neighborhood or workplace.

| Empathetic Learning[2]

In my own interfaith engagements, I have been greatly helped by a short document that is well known among those who are

1. Terry C. Muck, *Those Other Religions in Your Neighborhood: Loving Your Neighbor When You Don't Know How* (Grand Rapids: Zondervan, 1992).
2. Parts of this section are adapted from Richard J. Mouw, "Cultivating Intellectual Humility," in *Virtue and Vice*. Copyright © 2018 by Dr. Richard J. Mouw. Used by permission of Abilene Christian University Press.

actively engaged in the more professional kinds of interfaith dialogues: Leonard Swidler's "Dialogue Decalogue," where he sets forth ten principles for constructive interfaith engagement.[3] I won't get into all of Swidler's "commandments" here, but some of what he says applies nicely to talking with our neighbors. He emphasizes, for example, the need to approach perspectives different from our own with a humble spirit of learning. Understandably, this does not come easily for evangelicals, especially because we often focus almost exclusively on questions about salvation in discussing other religions. We have rightly insisted that humans can be reconciled to God only through the atoning work of Jesus Christ, and we have resisted any moves in the direction of religious relativism or syncretism.

Again, those concerns are crucial ones in thinking about other religions. But that should not keep us from asking whether we can gain insights into the truth about important matters by talking to persons of other faiths.

Underlying most of Swidler's commandments is the need for empathy, which is the ability to experience the feelings and concerns of others as if they were your own. I like to think of Christian empathy as a spiritual *hospitality*, a willingness to "make room" for the experiences and convictions of other people in our own hearts and minds. Indeed, we Christians have special advantages in nurturing this kind of hospitality. We know we are finite creatures. God is God, and we are not, which means that we fall far short of omniscience. And all of this is greatly exaggerated because of our sinful rebelliousness.

I personally am convinced that when we genuinely engage people of other faiths we sometimes receive some genuine spiritual insights from them. But even if some fellow evangelicals

3. "Dialogue Principles," Dialogue Institute and *Journal of Ecumenical Studies*, http://institute.jesdialogue.org/resources/tools/decalogue.

don't want to go that far with me on the subject, there ought to be no question that we can learn about how others have experienced the presence of Christians in their lives.

Here is a personal case in point. A rabbi once came to my presidential office at Fuller Seminary to discuss a project that he and I were involved in on First Amendment issues. We met for over an hour, and it was a good discussion. A week or so later he wrote me a note, thanking me for what had been an important encounter for him. He wanted to confess to me that he had dreaded coming to see me in my office. He had been raised in a small town in the Midwest—his was the only Jewish family in town. In the public school he attended, he said, the teacher would begin each day telling the students to "stand and say the prayer that our Lord Jesus taught us to say." He had been instructed by his rabbi at the synagogue his family attended in a nearby city that he was not to stand and say that prayer.

His nonparticipation in the daily act of prayer was noticeable, and in the schoolyard and on the way home from school the other kids often bullied him, calling him a "Christ killer." When he was told that he was to visit an evangelical seminary to meet with the president, those childhood fears were reawakened. When he arrived on Fuller's campus, he reported, "I broke out into a cold sweat!" And having told me his story, he thanked me for "making me feel safe with a Christian."

We Christians need to hear stories like that. In some cases we do have to overcome legitimate fears from people of other faith communities. We have often treated Jewish people horribly over the past two thousand years. And the Muslim community lives with memories of our past "crusades" against them. And it was Christian men who formed a vigilante group that murdered Joseph Smith, the founder of Mormonism, in the jailhouse in Carthage, Illinois.

We have some empathetic listening to do in our conversations with non-Christian folks. By hearing the stories of others, we can better understand ourselves as we do the necessary work to create the kinds of trusting relationships that will then be accepted by others when we talk to them about our faith in a loving Savior.

| Healing a High School Wound

On a Sunday evening in November 2004, I spoke for eight minutes from the podium at the Mormon Tabernacle in Salt Lake City. I will not go into all the details here regarding the event—I have written about it at some length elsewhere.[4] The basic facts of the story are that it was an event when Mormons and evangelicals were gathered together in large numbers to hear Ravi Zacharias speak about the essentials of the gospel. And I had been asked by our Mormon hosts to offer some introductory words.

What I said that evening turned out to be quite controversial in the evangelical world. I told the Mormons present that we evangelicals have often sinned against Mormons by telling the LDS what they believe rather than asking them. This event, I then explained, can be an important step in being more truthful and loving toward each other.

Again, many evangelicals found that repentant tone—"We have sinned against you"—to be deeply disturbing. Who did I think I was in taking it upon myself to apologize to Mormons on behalf of evangelicals?

I am still glad I said what I did. And while the angry reaction of some evangelicals did sting a bit, there was one email

4. See Richard J. Mouw, *Talking with Mormons: An Invitation to Evangelicals* (Grand Rapids: Eerdmans, 2012).

I received that more than compensated for the harsh attacks. It was from a Mormon university student who wrote it several hours after the Tabernacle event ended. She said that she was not able to sleep. She had been shedding tears of gratitude, and she wanted to tell me why.

In her first two years as a high school student she had formed a close friendship with two evangelical girls. They had noticed one day in the cafeteria that she bowed her head to pray before her meal, and they introduced themselves to her. From that point on they sat at lunch together, and they frequently met together before school began in the morning to read a passage from the Bible and pray for God's guidance during the day.

The two years of maintaining this friendship were for her, she said, a highlight of her early teenage years. But then one Monday her two friends came to her and told her that they no longer wanted anything to do with her. Over the weekend they had heard an evangelical countercult speaker/writer talk at their church about Mormonism. He had convinced them that Mormons are a deceptive cult who worship a false Jesus. They had heeded his warnings against taking what Mormons say about their faith at face value. So now they were cutting off their friendship ties with her.

This had been, she said, a major trauma for her. She loved Jesus and had been so encouraged by spending time with two friends who loved him also. During the next two years at that high school they avoided all contact with her. Those years for her were a time of spiritual loneliness and pain.

Our evening at the Tabernacle had been a profoundly emotional experience for her. To hear an evangelical say "We have sinned against you" to the Mormon community had begun several hours of emotional and spiritual healing for her. She was writing to express her gratitude.

I saw her message to me as a word of assurance that it had not been wrong for me to confess that evangelicals have sinned against Mormons. The bold declarations of Mormonism as satanic had wounded a young teenager who wanted to reach out to two other followers of Jesus. She did not deserve to be treated in that manner by her friends—and, more specifically, by leaders who encourage that kind of spirit.

The great G. K. Chesterton put it well when he observed that "idolatry is committed not merely by setting up false gods, but also by setting up false devils."[5] The best way to avoid bearing false witness regarding the beliefs of our neighbors is to be sure that we have listened carefully to their own accounts of those beliefs.

| Standing alongside Others

I am not a relativist who believes anything goes in theology. I care deeply about what I take to be the basic issues of life, especially when it comes to questions like who God is and what it takes for a person to get right with God. And I can't get far into a discussion of those questions without talking about Jesus as the heaven-sent Savior who went to the cross of Calvary to pay the debt for our sins and, having been raised from the dead, ascended to the heavenly throne from which he will someday return to appear on clouds of glory. I believe those things with all my heart, and I believe them because they are taught in the Bible, which is God's infallible Word to us, telling us all we need to know about God's will for our lives.

None of this cancels out, however, the need to approach others with a spirit of empathy, to try as much as possible to place

5. G. K. Chesterton, *Illustrated London News*, September 11, 1909; cited by "Quotations of G. K. Chesterton," American Chesterton Society, http://www.chesterton.org/quotations-of-g-k-chesterton.

ourselves within the perspective of the other person. Indeed, our confidence in the truth of the gospel can free us to probe the questions—the deep questions—the other person is asking, and explore with that person the degree to which their religious framework is capable of providing adequate, even compelling, answers to those questions.

An empathetic approach to persons of other faiths is, I believe, necessary in order to establish the trust that can make genuine communication possible. And this, in turn, means setting aside our much-too-common temptation to win rhetorical victories that cut off any interesting conversations—to say nothing of committing the sin of bearing false witness against our neighbors. The real goal of those conversations is for us to understand better how the gospel can reach into the hearts of people of other faiths—in the hope that we will gain the opportunity to witness to the ways in which that gospel has reached into our own heart with its saving and healing power.

| Another Case in Point

I need to push the case for empathy a little further by getting into another example. In February 2017, the planners of the National Prayer Breakfast in Washington, DC, sponsored a post-breakfast seminar on "Muslims and Jesus." I attended the event with about two hundred others. One of the Muslim panelists described himself as "a Muslim follower of Jesus." He assured us that he was indeed a devout Muslim. But, he testified, he also regularly reads the Gospel accounts of the life of Jesus. The New Testament, he said, has become an important part of his life because Jesus has added a dimension to his deeply held Muslim beliefs by teaching him lessons about love and forgiveness. Because of Jesus, he testified, "I have become a more loving and forgiving Muslim."

The audience for this panel was predominantly evangelical, and when the discussion was opened up for questions from the audience, someone immediately challenged the Muslim panelist: "But you Muslims deny the reality of the work of the cross! How can you say you follow Jesus when you deny what the New Testament says about his atoning work?"

The Muslim responded with an almost pleading tone: "Why do you Christian folks always go immediately to that topic? Yes, we Muslims have questions about whether the crucifixion of Jesus really happened. But why is that such a big deal for you?" Then he pointed to the person next to him, an evangelical missionary to the Middle East: "My Christian friend here has been preaching to Muslims about the cross for ten years, and what are his results? About six converts—six people in ten years! Now, if he had encouraged Muslims to read the Gospels to learn from Jesus about love and forgiveness, he would have thousands of Muslim people reading the New Testament!"

I was disappointed that the conversation so quickly took on an argumentative character. I wish it had gone differently. We could have asked the Muslim panelist to be more specific about why he found Jesus so engaging. How, in practical ways, do Jesus's teachings about love and forgiveness expand on what he finds in the Qur'an? In what distinct ways, if any, does Jesus speak to his deepest hopes and fears? At the very least we should want to keep the conversation going without putting anyone on the defensive with an accusatory challenge.

To be sure, we ought not to ignore the ways the message of the cross is a "stumbling block" to unbelievers (1 Cor. 1:23). However, we must also allow for the ways in which people can benefit from the redemptive mission completed at Calvary without being intellectually clear in their understanding of that mission. One real possibility, then, is that the Muslim panelist was not aware of the ways in which the love and forgiveness he was experiencing through Jesus is possible only because of what Jesus accomplished by his atoning work—that Jesus was actually speaking to a spiritual gap in the Muslim experience of God.

J. H. Bavinck was a Dutch theologian who was an expert on Islam. He observed that "in Islam there is little room for a life of personal fellowship with God. Allah is so great and so exalted, and his will is so completely dominating, that very little is left on the human side."[6] It should not surprise us, then, that Muslims might look to Jesus for something that goes beyond what Islam by itself has to offer.

The missionary-anthropologist Paul Hiebert influenced many with his distinction between "bounded sets" and "centered sets." It is very clear what belongs in a bounded set. The requirements for membership have to do with clearly definable characteristics: "apples" and "oranges" are bounded sets. A centered set, however, "is created by defining a center, and the relationship of things to that center. Some things may be far from the center, but they are moving towards the center, therefore, they are part of the centered set." But, Hiebert said, other "objects may be near the center but are moving away from it."[7]

How does this apply to our Muslim panelist? Well, we certainly cannot say with any degree of certainty that in terms of salvation he is "in." But his testimony about Jesus does open

---

6. J. H. Bavinck, "Defining Religious Consciousness: The Five Magnetic Points," in *The J. H. Bavinck Reader*, ed. John Bolt, James D. Bratt, and Paul J. Visser, trans. James A. De Jong (Grand Rapids: Eerdmans, 2013), 181.

7. Paul G. Hiebert, "Conversion, Culture and Cognitive Categories," *Gospel in Context* 1 (1978): 24–29.

up the possibility that he is moving toward rather than away from Jesus. This is another of those areas of theological interest where I am simply willing to live with some mystery—even as I know that it is important to keep the conversation going about the basics of the gospel.

11

The Mystery
of the Christian "Other"

A reporter interviewed me about my published views on Christian civility.[1] "You have worked at 'convicted civility' in a lot of settings," he said. "Where have you personally found it most difficult to be civil?" My answer: "Within the Christian community!" When I engage in lengthy dialogues with persons who are non-Christians, I don't feel defeated when I have not succeeded in changing their minds. I am a Calvinist. I know that the real change can come only by the power of the Holy Spirit. My responsibility in those conversations is to learn the lessons the Spirit wants me to absorb and to work at clearing up misconceptions about the Christian message. The Lord will use all of that according to his own purposes.

---

1. This section on Christian civility is adapted from Richard J. Mouw, "Cultivating Christian Civility," *The Banner*, June 16, 2016, https://www.thebanner .org/features/2016/06/cultivating-christian-civility. © 2016. *The Banner*, Christian Reformed Church in North America. All rights reserved. Used by permission.

But things are different within the Christian community. Here we expect regenerated hearts and minds to be clear about the truth. Confused theology—to say nothing of outright theological error—can cause serious damage in the life and mission of the church. There are eternally significant matters about which we cannot be content to simply agree to disagree.

Intrafaith Challenges

What all of that has meant for me in my journey is that I have had to work especially hard at intrafaith dialogue. On an ongoing basis my continuing struggle is with folks in the Religious Right. In my book on civility I acknowledged at one point that there are times when "civility" is not enough.[2] For me, those times show up most frequently when I encounter folks who claim the "evangelical" label while celebrating "biblical manhood," or when they espouse attitudes and policies that lend credibility to the public perception that evangelicals are homophobic, racist, and generally mean-spirited. For this I can only plead for prayers on my behalf, that I not generate my own brand of prejudicial harshness!

Another big—but less intense—challenge for me has been in what we typically label the "ecumenical" arena. I often have as many problems engaging with folks on my theological left as I do with folks on my right. I do like to think of myself as a moderate, but that does not mean I am always nice about it. I often find myself too reactionary in dealing with views of both more conservative and more liberal Christians. In working my way through intrafaith engagements, I find it necessary to keep reminding myself that I need to work on being in a learning mode.

2. Richard J. Mouw, *Uncommon Decency: Christian Civility in an Uncivil World*, 2nd ed. (Downers Grove, IL: InterVarsity, 2010), 135–47.

| Learning "Ecumenism"

A staff member from the World Council of Churches once spent a few days on Fuller Seminary's campus, and he met with me toward the end of his visit. He told me how impressed he was with what he had experienced. "A very vital Christian community," he said. "You have an excellent faculty, and your students are remarkably talented." But then he added a word of concern: "I just wish you folks were more ecumenically engaged!"

I refrained from telling him what I thought about his complaint. Fuller, I wanted to tell him, was probably the most ecumenical seminary in the world: students from 120 denominations and 70 nations, with significant numbers from mainline Protestant denominations here in the United States (Presbyterian, Methodist, Lutheran, Episcopal, Disciples of Christ, Baptists) and some Catholics. How do we get more ecumenical than that?

I knew, of course, what he meant by the label "ecumenical." He wished we were more organizationally connected to "conciliar ecumenism"—World Council of Churches, National Council of Churches, various official networks within the various confessional traditions.

I had known that world fairly well, having actively served for five years on the Faith and Order Commission of the National Council of Churches as a representative of the Christian Reformed Church, in one of the slots allotted to nonmember denominations. I made some good friends on that commission, and I even had a hand in writing a couple of the formal reports. But I can't say that I came away from the experience wishing that evangelicals in general would be more involved.

Indeed, my experience in conciliar ecumenism made me reluctant to accept the invitation from the Institute of Ecumenical and Cultural Research in Collegeville, Minnesota, to

participate in a weeklong seminar on "The Meaning of Ecumenism." But the executive director of the institute, Bob Bil-
heimer, prevailed upon me, and I agreed to attend. Bob had
come to Collegeville after several years in Geneva as one of the
World Council's leaders, and I was intrigued by his assurance
about the Collegeville discussion: "Don't worry—it won't be
like what goes on at the WCC or NCC!"

He was right. On the first day, after a round of introductions,
each of us was asked to describe an event where we had first
experienced ecumenism—with the explanation that by "ecumenism" we should understand being pleasantly surprised by
a good experience with someone from a part of the Christian
world that we had not previously looked upon with favor.

The experience that immediately came to mind for me, given
that understanding of "ecumenism," occurred when I "went
forward" at Billy Graham's evangelistic service at Madison
Square Garden in 1957. The practice at the meetings was for
Graham to pray over those gathered in front of him who had
accepted his evangelistic invitation, and then to encourage them
to spend a few minutes praying with volunteers who were at
that moment moving toward us to take us to a quieter place
for prayer and some words of encouragement. The man who
beckoned to me was wearing a clerical collar.

Clerical collars were not a part of the evangelical world in
which I was raised. Indeed, when we saw someone wearing
one, we immediately identified that with either Catholicism
or liberal Protestantism—neither being representative of the
kind of Christianity that we approved of.

For me to respond to an invitation to talk and pray with
someone wearing a clerical collar was itself a serious act of
faith for me. And it went well. The man—I think he told me his
first name, but I did not find out what church he represented—
spoke with genuine kindness to me about the love of Jesus, and

he prayed that the Lord would guide me as a teenager in my journey of faith.

That story was not out of line with others in the twenty or so folks gathered for the Collegeville consultation. All the testimonies were about very practical situations in which God had surprised each of us with positive encounters that stretched our previous understandings of who was in our circle of faith.

| Visible Unity[3]

I had come to the Collegeville discussions not only with memories of some negative experiences at the National Council of Churches but also with a history of hearing many evangelical criticisms of the conciliar brand of ecumenism. In my senior year at Houghton College, I followed through on that line of thought by doing some reading on the subject for a class paper I wrote. I long ago lost the paper, but I clearly remember relying heavily on a book-length treatment of the subject by Marcellus Kik, *Ecumenism and the Evangelical*, published in 1958. Kik was a Reformed pastor-theologian who had begun his seminary studies at Princeton but then transferred to Westminster Theological Seminary when J. Gresham Machen left the Princeton faculty in 1929 to establish the new school in Philadelphia.

Kik's arguments against organizational "church unity" made good sense to me at the time, and indeed they have had a lasting influence on my thinking on the subject. When I reread his book several years ago, I was surprised how well I had remembered the actual formulation of his key argument, which focused on both the organizational efficiency and missional effectiveness of

3. Parts of this section are adapted from Richard J. Mouw, "Response to Dr. Reno," in *The Gospel of John: Theological-Ecumenical Readings*, ed. Charles Raith II (Eugene, OR: Wipf and Stock, 2017), 158–67. Used by permission of Wipf and Stock.

small denominations. "Often the smaller denominations," he argued, "evidence greater activity in casting out devils prevalent in the world, than do the larger denominations. In Christian work quality counts far more than quantity." Then he appealed to the example of ancient Israel, where "for more effective organization and efficiency the Lord divided the small nation of Israel into 12 tribes, each having its own government." When the Israelites wanted a human king to give them a more visible unity, he said, God was displeased with them "and finally caused division into two kingdoms. . . . One wonders how much of the nature of the ancient Israelite is in the ecumenical movement with its passion for a visible central government."[4]

Kik did also get around to acknowledging, however, that there is indeed a biblical mandate for working toward Christian unity, citing Christ's high-priestly prayer in John 17 "that they might all be one." He then went on to argue at length that true unity must mirror, in accordance with Christ's prayer, the unity between the Father and the Son, which is a unity, he says, of doctrine, of purpose, and of love.[5] Unless these conditions are met, we will have only a false unity. I still agree with that. The "visible unity" schemes that have often been set forth in the mainline ecumenical movement are deficient when they fail to acknowledge the doctrinal and missional concerns touched on in the John 17 prayer.

It's easy to use the defects of many "visible unity" efforts simply to live with the status quo of our divisions. What I learned at Collegeville was to take some steps of faith toward cultivating a genuine desire to *search* for a basis for unity. For me the search took concrete shape in the form of two friendships that I formed there. One was with Margaret O'Gara, a Catholic

4. J. Marcellus Kik, *Ecumenism and the Evangelical* (Philadelphia: P&R, 1958), 23.

5. Kik, *Ecumenism*, 42–44.

theologian who regularly expressed her disapproval of some of my theological formulations. The other was Anthony Ugolnik, a Russian Orthodox layman who was later to become a priest, who seemed to be coming from a totally different religious universe than the one I inhabited. I can still remember feeling eager to get back to Grand Rapids, Michigan, where I could tell my fellow Dutch Calvinists about all the strange things I had heard from these two individuals.

A funny thing happened to me over the next several months after first being with these two, however. From time to time, one of my fellow Calvinists—a faculty colleague or a preacher—would refer to something related to either Catholicism or Orthodoxy that I knew was not a fair representation of the views I had heard from my two Collegeville friends. When I agreed to return to the institute the next summer for another round of discussions, it was with a new kind of eagerness: I could not wait to tell my two newfound dialogue partners about the misinformed things I had heard some Grand Rapids people say about their two traditions. Those two became close Christian friends from whom I have learned much.

| Celebrating Perplexity

The account that I have just given of that stage in my own ecumenical formation displays some key evangelical themes. For one thing, I have represented it as a kind of conversion experience, which is a favorite evangelical motif. But I also linked the emergence of my ecumenical consciousness to very personal encounters. What this means, I suggest, is that the presence of *desire* is of the utmost importance. We may not know exactly where our conversations will lead us, but we have to *want* to keep at it.

The lessons I learned from the two friends I have described were each quite different. O'Gara was a deeply committed Catholic, but she expressed her Catholic convictions with a decidedly "evangelical" tone. She loved the older evangelical hymns and put them to good use in her own spiritual journey. For example, I once attended a meeting of the National Workshop on Christian Unity while she served as the organization's president. The speaker at one of the plenary sessions was a very liberal theologian who in his speech criticized a statement of the World Council of Churches because it referred to God as "Lord." Lordship, he said, was a much too "hierarchical" image, encouraging the unhealthy picture of a universe in which God is "up there" and we have to submit to a "patriarchal rule."

I was sitting with O'Gara in the front row, and I whispered to her, "This is awful." She responded, "I know. But be patient, Richard. As president, I get to pick the hymns." When the session came to an end, she went to the podium and invited the audience to sing "How Great Thou Art" before the benediction. I will never forget her smile to me as she led the group in the singing of the words of that hymn celebrating the wondrous transcendence of God. Now that she is in heaven, I picture her still singing that song.

Ugolnik was a more difficult case for me theologically. He was a passionate advocate for the idea that the Orthodox Church is the only community that deserves to be called "church." There really cannot be any actual divisions *within* the church, he would argue, because Orthodoxy alone is "the one, holy, catholic and apostolic Church." The only true path to unity, then, is for the rest of us to become Orthodox. Needless to say, that is quite hard for an evangelical to take. But I never sensed any spiritual arrogance in Tony. He clearly saw O'Gara and myself as fellow Christians with whom he shared deep bonds.

So, how do I account for my own sense of a deep unity in Christ with people whose views are in opposition to my own on some key theological topics? Well, the reason why I have told all of this was to get to this point, where I can give Ugolnik the punchline. In a piece that he wrote about our Collegeville experiences, he described the lesson he learned from the rest of us in this way: "We need to be perplexed together. We need to rediscover the humility to be puzzled, the courage to engage the ambiguities and conundrums in our texts and look to each other to find the flashes and refractions of answers in places we least expect them."[6]

I have made positive use of the word "mystery" in these pages. But here Ugolnik's "perplexed" is much more fitting. To be perplexed is to experience mystery—but there is more. Perplexity is mystery mixed with puzzlement. My wife and I can experience the mystery of a beautiful sunset together without being puzzled about how we can share in the mystery together. My two friends and I found one another perplexing precisely because we disagreed on serious matters while we clearly shared in a sense of mystery at the wonders of the gospel. My perplexity about them—and about many other Christian "others" whom I have met along the way—has been a source of joy for me.

| The Role of Trust[7]

I have complained a bit here about my time on the Faith and Order Commission of the National Council of Churches, so I

6. Tony Ugolnik, quoted in Patrick Henry, "Ecumenical Gift Exchange: A Triumvirate of Collegeville Institute Greats," *Bearings Online*, June 29, 2017, https://collegevilleinstitute.org/bearings/ecumenical-gift-exchange/.

7. Parts of this section have been adapted from Mouw, "Response to Dr. Reno," 158–67. Used by permission of Wipf and Stock.

should also report on one of the good experiences I had during that term of service. As I mentioned earlier, I spent those five years as a member of the commission, representing the Christian Reformed Church in one of the commission's "nonmember denomination" slots. At one session, I took a seat next to a good friend, Father Robert Stephanopoulos, at the time the dean of the Greek Orthodox cathedral in Cleveland. As I looked down the row, I noticed that each of us in that row represented nonmember church communities: Christian Reformed, Greek Orthodox, Missouri Synod Lutheran, and Roman Catholic. I whispered to Bob, "Look at this row of people. We could leave and have our own discussion about Christian unity." He responded, "Maybe we should. It would be a more heated discussion. But at least we would be dealing with the right question: What does it mean to represent communions where it makes good sense to talk about being 'the one true Church'?"

A "heated discussion" indeed. But an important one—the kind of conversation that could be productive if we genuinely accepted one another as dialogue partners without being put off by our diverse theologies about "church." That would, of course, require a lot of trust. My Collegeville experience helped me to discover that. It forced me to stick with a conversation with folks—Catholics and Orthodox—whom evangelicals have typically not seriously engaged in theological discussion.

Our evangelical selectivity in choosing conversation partners has often allowed us to maintain our caricatures and stereotypes. By resisting engagement with others in more inclusive settings for dialogue, we miss out on opportunities to better understand other Christians—and even worse, we promote the conditions in which we continually commit the sin of bearing false witness against our Christian neighbors.

What my Collegeville experience also exemplifies is that more intimate, face-to-face sustained discussions accomplish more in correcting these sinful tendencies than do large, official discussions among church leaders. A healthier quest for Christian unity will foster this more sustained face-to-face mode of exchange.

I have long admired C. S. Lewis's use of the phrase "surprised by joy" to characterize his spiritual journey. I don't plan to write a similar account of my own journey, but if I did, I think I would choose for my title "surprised by perplexity."

12

Public Activism

There is some perplexity, of course, that does not bring joy. It is a state of troubled puzzlement. This is pretty much my condition of mind and heart regarding what many evangelicals have been saying and doing in the public square in recent years.

With all the complaints these days about how evangelicals have become too politicized, it takes some effort to remember that there was a time, as recently as four decades ago, when evangelical Christians were regularly criticized for being "apolitical." Due to a variety of factors in the early decades of the twentieth century—the liberal takeover of major Protestant denominations, the cultural influence of evolutionist thinking, the breakdown of moral standards influenced by biblical thought—evangelicals became increasingly pessimistic about the possibilities for significant social reform.

This pessimistic outlook prevailed for over a half century, encouraging evangelicals to concentrate primarily on helping individuals to prepare their souls for the hereafter. Perspectives on the larger culture were characterized by the kind of apocalyptic imagery made popular by the nineteenth-century evangelist Dwight L. Moody. The American ship is sinking, Moody had proclaimed; the only task left is to urge individuals to scramble into the lifeboats—the enclaves of "Bible-believing Christians"—to await the heavenly rescue operation. Or, to cite an oceanic metaphor that I heard much in my evangelical childhood: prior to the return of Christ, trying to do some good by means of social-political engagement is like rearranging the deck chairs on the *Titanic*.

My own initial forays into political activism took place in the 1960s, when I got caught up in the civil rights movement and protests against the Vietnam War. It was a lonely time to be an evangelical. People who had been my spiritual heroes were now suggesting that Martin Luther King Jr. was being used by the communists, and that God was on the side of those who supported our military policies in Southeast Asia. I was restless to find a spiritual home where the causes that I had come to care about were taken seriously. I attended more liberal churches, but the kind of preaching I heard there made me even more restless to move on from that brand of Protestantism. I studied the great social documents from the Vatican and learned much from them, but I never seriously considered a spiritual crossing of the Tiber.

My restlessness eventually led me back to evangelicalism, where I discovered that there were others in my generation who had attempted to move on from evangelicalism for the same factors that had vexed me. Fortunately, we found each other, and things took a wonderful turn when about forty of us gathered at a downtown Chicago YMCA in 1973 to produce a document called "The Chicago Declaration of Evangelical Social Concerns." We were joined by several of the older generation as well—Carl Henry, Frank Gabelein, Paul Rees, and others. Dick Ostling of *Time* magazine remarked that this was likely the first time in the twentieth century when forty evangelical leaders got together for a whole weekend to discuss issues of social concern.[1]

We younger folks were aware that some of our elders—Carl Henry in particular—were a bit nervous about some of the themes we insisted on addressing. But it was clear that they knew we were onto some issues that had long been neglected, and they did want to give us their blessing. Apart from the specifics we touched on, the main message was that some new evangelical voices were calling for an activism that focused on issues of justice and peace.

This new evangelical activism received additional national attention when Jimmy Carter, in campaigning for the presidency in 1976, identified himself as an evangelical. *Newsweek* magazine then declared in a cover story that 1976 was "The Year of the Evangelical."

In a few years, though, a very different sort of activism made its appearance when the new Religious Right became a political force in the 1980s. The most prominent of the movements in that brand of activism was the Moral Majority. And while that group no longer exists, the Religious Right is still a very visible voting bloc on the current political scene. The result is that these days evangelicals are very engaged in social-political life. Regrettably, however, we are not particularly clear about what it means to engage the larger culture in ways that are biblically faithful.

1. This remark was made to Ron Sider, who reported it in his book *Good News and Good Works: A Theology for the Whole Gospel* (Grand Rapids: Baker Books, 1993), 20. See also Richard J. Mouw, "Awakening the Evangelical Conscience," *Christianity Today*, October 1, 2006, https://www.christianitytoday.com/history /issues/issue-92/awakening-evangelical-conscience.html.

| Engagement[2]

The word "engage" actually has two very different popular senses, neither of which I would want to own as my stance toward culture. There is the courtship sense, as when couples get engaged. That sense of engagement is an intimate one. It is to commit to marriage—the union of two persons for better or for worse. That kind of engagement is wonderful for couples in love, but it is not proper for Christians in their relation to the larger culture. To commit to a "marriage" between Christian faith and the culture in which we find ourselves is a dangerous thing.

The other sense is an image used in warfare. When a military unit engages an enemy force, the result is violent conflict. This is the sense in which Christian "culture warriors" go about engaging the larger culture. They see the relationship as one of confronting an enemy. That also strikes me as a wrongheaded approach to the larger society.

In the years immediately following the Chicago Declaration, we younger types began to explore the theological resources necessary for our social activism. Some gravitated toward the version of Anabapist thought developed by John Howard Yoder in his *Politics of Jesus*. Others drew inspiration from the Lutheran theologian Dietrich Bonhoeffer, who had been martyred during the Nazi era. Still others looked to the witness of nineteenth-century Wesleyanism.

My own approach, which I began to develop in those early years in the 1970s, is strongly influenced by the nineteenth-century Dutch neo-Calvinist tradition, as set forth by Abraham Kuyper and Herman Bavinck. They were not only fine

2. Parts of this section are adapted from Richard J. Mouw, "Getting the Trophies Ready: Serving God in the Business World," *Journal of Markets & Morality* 18, no. 1 (Spring 2015): 189–98.

theologians of a decidedly evangelical sort, but they were active in Dutch political life, with Kuyper actually serving a term as the prime minister of the Netherlands.

Each of them viewed political life through the theological lens provided by their doctrine of common grace. They derived this doctrine from comments made by the great Reformer of the sixteenth century, John Calvin. Even though he had established himself as a defender of the doctrine of the "total depravity" of fallen humanity, he also managed to express appreciation on many occasions for the contributions of non-Christian thinkers. Before his evangelical conversion, Calvin had studied law, and he never lost his respect for the ideas he had gleaned from the writings of various Greek and Roman writers, especially Seneca. In his *Institutes* Calvin observes that there is an "admirable light of truth shining" in the thoughts of pagan thinkers. And this means that "the mind of man, though fallen and perverted from its wholeness," can still be "clothed and ornamented with God's excellent gifts." Indeed, he insists, to refuse to accept the truth produced by such minds is "to dishonor the Spirit of God."[3]

Of course, some of the things we might attribute to common grace—a disposition of divine favor toward unbelievers—can be attributed to the way God works, as Kuyper puts it, in "external" ways in the lives of non-Christians.[4] God sends rain to nurture the crops of both believing and unbelieving farmers. And even very wicked governments often manage to do some things that promote human flourishing. All of that can be explained simply by the work of divine providence—God using bent sticks to draw a few straight lines.

3. John Calvin, *Institutes of the Christian Religion*, ed. John T. McNeill, trans. Ford Lewis Battles (Philadelphia: Westminster, 1960), 2.3.6, p. 273.

4. Abraham Kuyper, "Common Grace," in *Abraham Kuyper: A Centennial Reader*, ed. James D. Bratt (Grand Rapids: Eerdmans, 1998), 181.

But Kuyper also sees God's Spirit operating "inside" of unbelievers, as does Calvin when he insists that the ancient pagans actually produced good *ideas* on occasion, out of a love for *truth*. Kuyper extends this notion to cultural life in general, describing the "inside" working of God's Spirit in human lives in other areas of interaction: common grace is at work "wherever civic virtue, a sense of domesticity, natural love, the practice of human virtue, the improvement of the public conscience, integrity, mutual loyalty among people, and a feeling for piety leaven life."[5]

That important emphasis of Kuyper is also affirmed by his younger colleague Herman Bavinck, who writes that because of common grace there is "sometimes a remarkable sagacity . . . given to [unbelievers] whereby they are not only able to learn certain things, but also to make important inventions and discoveries, and to put these to practical use in life."[6]

These three thinkers—Calvin, Kuyper, Bavinck—had deep convictions about the tragic effects of sin on all human life. Their understanding of depravity is that it is *total*—it affects all aspects of our lives. But that is not the same as affirming *absolute* depravity—the teaching that every thought and deed of the sinful heart and mind is worthless in the sight of God. Their perspective, then, calls for discernment. In political life this means that we should look for signs of justice and righteousness "out there" in the world, in the thoughts and actions of people who do not acknowledge the reality of the God whose designs they may be serving on occasion without acknowledging the nature and source of those designs.

Political engagement for Christians, then, should mean careful listening to those who do not share our faith. This

5. Kuyper, "Common Grace," 181.
6. Herman Bavinck, "Calvin and Common Grace," trans. *Geerhardus Vos, Princeton Theological Review* 7 (1909): 437–65, here 455; available online at http://www.monergism.com/thethreshold/sdg/pdf/bavinck_commongrace.pdf.

leads us to the kind of cooperation that Francis Schaeffer referred to as "co-belligerence," the forming of ad hoc alliances with people who profess other worldviews, but with whom we might share goals and strategies on specific issues in public life.[7]

| Governmental Authority

Now the big question: How do we actually *do* this in the public realm? What are the proper patterns of the Christian exercise of political power? The underlying issue that has to be addressed in this regard is the question of what government is *for*. What are the divine purposes that the exercise of political authority is meant to serve in collective human life?

One rather straightforward answer is the one that I learned early on in one of the first courses dealing with political topics that I took as an undergraduate in an evangelical college. We read an essay by the Calvinist philosopher Gordon Clark, who wrote that God established governments after the fall because of the need to control "a large number of evil people working at cross purposes."[8] What seems to be going on in that comment is a central focus on the apostle Paul's teaching in Romans 13, that governments have been ordained by God to exercise the power of the sword.

I certainly have no quarrel with Paul on this matter. He was writing in the context of the Roman Empire, whose rulers Christians rightly saw not only as pagan but also as overtly hostile to the convictions and practices of the Christian community. Even under these unfortunate political conditions, Paul

---

7. Francis Schaeffer, *Plan for Action: An Action Alternative Handbook for "Whatever Happened to the Human Race?"* (New York: Revell, 1980), 68.

8. Gordon Clark, *A Christian View of Men and Things* (Grand Rapids: Eerdmans, 1952), 146.

is insisting, we must respect the ways in which governments serve the will of God by exercising an ordering function.

It would be wrong to conclude from this, however, that every government that has authority over Christian citizens should be seen primarily in terms of serving God's righteous ordering purposes. Take the obvious case of Nazi Germany in the 1930s and '40s. Suppose Dietrich Bonhoeffer, who recoiled in horror at the actions of Hitler and his cronies—a repugnance that eventually led him to martyrdom—had read Romans 13:1–5 as applying to his own historical context in this way:

> Let every person be subject to the Nazi regime; for there is no authority except from God, and the authority of the Nazi regime has been instituted by God. Therefore whoever resists the Nazi regime resists what God has appointed, and those who resist the Nazi regime will incur judgment. The Nazi regime is not a terror to good conduct, but to bad. Do you wish to have no fear of the Nazi regime? Then do what is good, and you will receive its approval; for the Nazi regime is God's servant for your good. But if you do what is wrong, you should be afraid, for the Nazi regime does not bear the sword in vain! It is the servant of God to execute wrath on the wrongdoer. Therefore one must be subject to it, not only because of wrath but also because of conscience.

This obviously does not work. We rightly praise Bonhoeffer's active resistance to the horrors of Nazism, even as we also celebrate the heroic witness of Martin Luther King Jr. and others in their refusal to submit to the racist laws of the segregated American South.

Furthermore, those examples of civil disobedience seem to conform to actual examples we find in the Scriptures. During their Babylonian captivity, for example, Daniel and the men who went to the fiery furnace, insisting on fidelity to God's commands, were willing to face imprisonment and even death rather than obey an unjust law. Similarly, the Christian disciples in the book of Acts endure imprisonment for refusing to submit to mandates that they cease the proclamation of their message.

One move that Christian defenders of civil disobedience have made is to place these examples alongside other New Testament teaching in a kind of dialectical tension, calling for a balancing act of sorts. We must, they say, accept both Romans 13 and Revelation 13, the latter being a chapter depicting a blasphemous government, portrayed as a "beast," who claims authority over all humanity and is obeyed by all the citizens—except for those who are loyal to Christ ("the Lamb"). This sort of move is certainly motivated by the right kinds of concerns. But my own preference is to go beyond a mere dialectical tension, where Romans 13 is taken to be issuing a straightforward call for Christians to obey their governments, which must then be balanced off by a different sort of emphasis found in these other biblical references. Not content with a dialectical solution, I have searched for an interpretation of Romans 13 that coheres better with the other texts.

This more cohesive interpretation can be found by seeing Paul as setting forth a "normative" view of government, wherein the apostle is describing the relationship of a Christian citizen to a *properly functioning* political authority. On this interpretation, the reason why Romans 13 should not have been taken as mandating obedience to the Nazi regime is that the Nazis were not conforming to the norms for good government as set forth in that very Romans passage. The reason why Christian citizens ought to submit to the authority of a government, Paul is saying, is that God institutes governments for the purpose of being "God's servant for . . . good" (Rom. 13:4). A proper divinely instituted government will not cause "terror for those who do right, but for those who do wrong" (13:3). When we are given such a government, we can do "what is right, and [we] will be commended" (13:3). But when we are faced with a government that does the opposite of what Romans 13 describes—a government that rewards those who do evil and punishes those who do good—then we must not honor that government as God-ordained. The problem with the Nazi regime, then, was that it was not conforming to the standards that inform God's purposes in instituting political authority. In that case, it was not Bonhoeffer who was violating the norms set forth in Romans 13—it was the Nazi regime!

| A Power That Nurtures[9]

The Presbyterians in seventeenth-century Scotland had an interesting image that they liked to use about political authority. The political leader, they said, must be a "nursing father." These folks drew heavily from the Old Testament in expressing their political views. Their God was a divine Ruler who wanted his chosen people, his new Israel, to conform to standards not unlike those that he required of the ancient Israelites.

In the midst of some of the harsh rhetoric that they employed in their use of Old Testament language, they came up with this "nursing father" image. Here they were expressing Old Testament loyalties, drawing on some obscure imagery that is used on only a few occasions in the King James Version of the Old Testament. The breast-feeding image is applied to royalty twice in the book of Isaiah, and these Calvinist writers undoubtedly had these references in mind: "And kings shall be thy nursing fathers, and their queens thy nursing mothers" (49:23); "Thou . . . shalt

9. The following section is adapted from Richard J. Mouw, *Praying at Burger King* (Grand Rapids: Eerdmans, 2007), 121–23. Used with permission.

suck the breast of kings" (60:16). This is not the kind of imagery that most preachers these days would choose to feature in their sermon titles. But it is not a bad idea to keep it in mind. Here is the basic point: *God wants political leaders to be nurturers.*

Psalm 72 uses a slightly different nurturing image. The description here is of a righteous king: "May he be like rain falling on a mown field, like showers watering the earth" (v. 6). This is said in a context where the psalm writer is celebrating sustenance for the citizenry. This is not about literal food handouts, of course—although that may be required in some circumstances. The feeding here is a nurturing spirit that cares about the well-being of all the people, with special attention to "the needy." Governments are obliged by God to foster a climate of peace and righteousness for all the people.

Obviously, there is much to debate here about what this means in terms of practical policy. Those are good debates to have. I have changed my mind on policy matters many times in my adult life—and I continue to argue these matters, not only with other people but also even in my own mind and heart. The issues of public peace and righteousness are complex ones. And unlike many of my Calvinist ancestors, I know I have to cultivate a healthy spirit of toleration in the pluralistic society in which I live. But I do want governments to nurture, to promote a caring spirit, and to call all of us to recognize the need to work for a common good.

| Size Matters[10]

During a question-and-answer session after a public lecture I gave on a college campus, a student asked me whether I am in

10. The following section is adapted from Richard J. Mouw, "Government: Does Size Matter?," *Religion News Service*, April 25, 2017, https://pantheon-live

favor of "big government or small government." I told her that I have a difficult time answering that question. A lot hangs on how we assess a government's job performance. Most of us would agree that at the very least a state should provide a police force and military protection for its citizens. Maintaining streets and highways also seems to be a necessary government service. Attention also must be given to public safety measures: parents whose kids walk to neighborhood schools should be grateful for stop signs, traffic lights, speed zones, and crossing guards.

I personally would add several other things to the list. I enjoy state and national parks, and I am grateful for what governments do to make them possible. I want laws that prevent child and spousal abuse. I support consumer safety regulations. I enjoy museums and public radio. And even many of the most consistent advocates of small government rightly insist on a government-sponsored safety net to provide health care for the poorest and neediest of our fellow citizens.

In short, I find myself quickly going beyond the limits set by those who speak most loudly about "getting the government out of our lives." I acknowledge, of course, that legitimate arguments can—and should—be carried on about many specifics. When can a given service be most effectively provided by nongovernment groups and agencies? When does a top-heavy governmental bureaucracy itself become a detriment to the common good? These are important questions that must be debated.

The underlying issue here, though, are the questions: What are governments *for*? What is their basic role in collective human life?

In the Christian tradition, those who have argued for serious limitations on the functions of the state have portrayed government primarily as a remedy for our human sinfulness. But I still hold out for some more positive—nurturing—functions of government.

Obviously it takes some work to decide what this may mean for our present situation. And the effort requires a good dose of humility. The issues are complex ones, but we should work on them with the knowledge that God wants governments to nurture, to promote human flourishing in appropriate ways. That surely means that governments should not get so big that they hinder our ability to flourish as human beings—but neither should we want them to be too small!

| Patient but Active[11]

As I was growing up in evangelicalism, I often heard preachers talk about "the time of God's patience." They used it to encourage us to repent while there is still an opportunity for sinners to get right with God. When human history comes to an end and the great judgment day arrives, they said, there will be no more divine patience. We will be stuck with our basic choices—for or against salvation—for all eternity.

Those calls to repentance still shape my basic spiritual outlook. But when I participated in dialogues with Mennonites in the 1970s about political engagement, I heard them use "the time of God's patience" in a somewhat different way. It is not our task as Christians, they said, to eliminate all the evils in the world. That will happen only when God decides to bring things to the final culmination. In the meantime, we live in the

11. Parts of this section are adapted from Richard J. Mouw, "Divine Patience in Confused Times," *Religion News Service*, March 20, 2017, https://religion news.com/2017/03/20/divine-patience-in-confused-times. Copyright 2018 Religion News Service LLC. Republished with permission of Religion News Service LLC, all rights reserved.

time of God's patience. That's not a reason simply to accept the social and political status quo. We need to be witnesses for peace and justice, speaking truth to those who are in power.

Our calling for the present is not to be successful in the political realm. There is no room in the Christian community for messianic complexes. We already have a wonderfully all-sufficient Messiah, and we await his return with patience. But we also act. Jeremiah did not tell the ancient Israelites that they should bring about the full *shalom* of the city in which they were being held captive. Rather, the Lord wanted them to *seek* the *shalom*. The apostle Peter renews this mandate for the New Testament church: "Live such good lives among the pagans," he writes, so "that, though they accuse you of doing wrong, they may see your good deeds and glorify God on the day he visits us" (1 Pet. 2:12). This is a mandate that calls for a renewed discipleship in contemporary political life.

| The Teaching Role[12]

In the next chapter I am going to talk about the need for a renewed spiritual formation in equipping ourselves for taking our obligations as citizens seriously. I am increasingly convinced that the failures of contemporary evangelicalism in the public square are due to a lack of a proper *catechesis*, the broad *teaching* ministry of the church that goes beyond what happens in weekly worship services.

I am frequently invited to add my name as an endorser of a position paper on some topic of public concern. These days,

---

12. Parts of this section are adapted from Richard J. Mouw, "Why I Decline to Sign 'Prophetic' Declarations," *Religion News Service*, December 7, 2017, https://religionnews.com/2017/12/07/why-i-decline-to-sign-prophetic-declarations/. Copyright 2018 Religion News Service LLC. Republished with permission of Religion News Service LLC, all rights reserved.

more often than not, I decline to be a signatory, even though I often actually agree with what the declaration says. Sometimes it is a call—usually issued by academics and/or church leaders—for peacemaking. Or it is a petition about some justice concern. I typically read the statement carefully. Often I get the impression that the only folks who will read the document carefully are like-minded people. The declaration may be framed as "speaking truth to power," but it is fairly obvious that the in-power types will really pay no attention. The drafters of the petition may realize that, but they take seriously an obligation to be prophetic.

While I talked a lot about being "prophetic" in my early days of social activism, I don't use that word much these days. A while back I did a word search on my laptop files for everything I have written over the past couple of decades, and I did not find myself at any point explicitly advocating being prophetic. When I have used the word at all, I have typically been quoting other people, or discussing biblical prophetic literature, or arguing with my Mormon friends about whether a church these days has to be headed up by someone who is officially labeled "prophet."

A cynic might suggest that having served for two recent decades as a seminary president, I was attempting to raise money in circles where being prophetic does not attract donors with considerable giving capacity. I have tried to stay honest with myself about that possibility.

But I do have what I consider to be some good theological reasons for avoiding engagement in prophetic activity. In ancient Israel there was often a tension between the prophets on the one hand and the kings and priests on the other hand. In the New Testament, though, there is no clear call for leaders to function as prophets. Indeed, a solid theological tradition says that the three offices of prophet, priest, and king have come together in Jesus. My own inclination is to say, then, that once God has brought something together in Christ we should never separate them out again. The role of *teacher* seems to have become more important—as the Catholic Church recognizes in emphasizing the importance of the magisterium. And the Catholic Church explicitly recognizes that one test of the effectiveness of a doctrinal statement is whether it is "received." Was the doctrine clearly stated? Has it been seen as important to the life of the believing community? Does it lend itself to confusion or to clarity about what is intended?

I don't question that there are moments in history—Nazi Germany is an obvious case in point—when we have no choice but to utter unqualified prophetic verdicts. In those contexts we are compelled to proclaim a bold "No!" to a specific state of affairs, even if in doing so we are voices crying in the wilderness. But outside those extreme situations it is dangerous to see ourselves as simply making pronouncements. If we have something important to say, we should pay careful attention to how best to bring people to see things our way. Actually, when we see functioning as prophets as our only recourse, we may want to ask whether we got to that point because we have failed in our teaching efforts.

Those of us who get paid to teach students know that when we plan an introductory course in some important area of the intellectual life, we do not say everything we know in the first lecture. Students need to be invited into an exploration of new and/or difficult subject matter, and they need to be instructed in the basics before getting into the complexities. An effective teacher does not say everything she knows on the first day. Good teaching consists not simply in saying true things but also in leading people into the truth, even if that takes some time. And much can be gained by emphasizing, wherever possible, the continuity between the new areas of learning and what students already are convinced of.

And classroom teachers even need to be a little careful with the idea of "leading people into the truth." We are all learners. Some of the best courses I have taught have been ones where I came away with the sense that I learned as much as—maybe even more than—my students.

Much the same can be said for the public teaching role—as exercised by academics, pastors, denominational officials, lay leaders, and the like. Our public pedagogy requires a measure of empathy and reassurance toward those whom we want to influence—as well as a humble recognition that we ourselves are learners! I find these characteristics are often missing in those religious leaders who emphasize the need for "prophetic" statements on various topics. If our goal is simply to say a lot of true things, then we can take comfort that we have performed our prophetic responsibilities when we issue straightforward public statements that come off as critical, say, of the concerns of many other religious folks. But if our assignment is to teach the truth, then we have a more difficult—and more highly nuanced—task. Good teaching requires patience—a trait that we don't often associate with prophets.

Patience is, of course, one of those spiritual qualities listed in the old King James Version of Romans 5:4. More contemporary translations substitute "character" (e.g., NIV, NRSV) or "strength of character" (NLT). In a Christian community, we are all in need of the formation that promotes that kind of strength—not the least being for our engagement in the public square.

| 13 |

Spiritual Formation
for Political Discipleship

As I said in the previous chapter, in the aftermath of the 1973
Chicago Declaration some of us realized that the kind of activism we were calling for had to be sustained by solid theological
resources. This was for me an exciting time, when a public
conversation about evangelical social concerns was directly connected to my own scholarly pursuits. What I eventually came
to realize, however, was that as important as the theological
dimension is, it must also be intimately connected to a more
practical kind of spiritual formation.

| The Institutional Church's Role

Evangelicals have often been presented with a false choice about
our role in public life. We either completely withdraw from
trying to influence things, or we initiate "takeover" programs.
There is an alternative pattern, though, one that I believe is
mandated by Scripture: in the present time, where the fullness

of Christ's kingdom is not yet with us, we are called to do what we can in the political realm, given the opportunities and abilities that God provides for us in the places where the Lord calls us to be faithful.

In saying that, I have to make it clear that I do not mean to argue that the institutional churches—local congregations or denominational agencies—should make it their business regularly to pronounce on the specifics of public policy. I place a strong emphasis on the importance of Christian organizations that are a step away from the worshiping church community in addressing specific areas of public life. I follow Abraham Kuyper in this regard, in his important distinction between the institutional church and the church as organism. The institutional church gathers for such things as worship (preaching, sacraments), catechesis, and spiritual formation. But the people of God need to gather for other purposes as well, beyond the borders of the institutional church as such. The evangelical world has long fostered, for example, vocationally specific groups, such as the Christian Legal Society, Full Gospel Business chapters, and the Fellowship of Christian Athletes. Similar groups have formed to promote Christian perspectives on public policy matters: Right to Life, Evangelicals for Social Action, the Center for Public Justice, Focus on the Family. The institutional church should see itself as sending us forth into Christian discernment discussions regarding the various spheres of human interaction in the larger world in which we find ourselves on a daily basis.

This distinction between the institutional church and what we evangelicals call parachurch avoids the false choice that is posed when we assume that either "the church" speaks out on political topics or Christians are left on their own when they make their way as individuals in their daily lives. The effective alternative is for Christians, having heard the call to discipleship in their worshiping communities, to get together with other

Christians who share common concerns, to seek discernment together for important areas of life in the larger culture. The institutional church should promote those intermediate communal discussions as a step away from the local church but also a step prior to purely individual discipleship. It is in those communities of discernment where I am convinced that much of the details of political life are best addressed.

I accept Kuyper's distinction between the church as institute and the church as organism because I think it is good theology. But even without that, the distinction has practical value. The work of pastors and other church leaders is complex, and we should not expect them to have expertise on issues of public policy. It makes more sense for the application of the church's teaching to political specifics to be dealt with in contexts where those matters are addressed by those who have the interest and expertise to reflect on the meaning of discipleship for political life.

What then *is* the role of the institutional church regarding political life? To argue that pastors and other church leaders do not have an obligation to address political specifics is not to remove politics as such from the church's agenda. Having spent decades emphasizing the call to evangelical action in the social-political realm, as well as working on important theological topics bearing on political life and thought, I have come to see the importance of nurturing the kind of spiritual formation necessary for engagement in political life.

| Changing Hearts[1]

One of the themes we often heard from evangelicals during the civil rights movement in the 1960s was that trying to legislate

---

1. Parts of this section are adapted from Richard J. Mouw, "How to Change Hearts on Race," *Religion News Service*, January 13, 2018, https://religionnews

morality was misguided. "Only changed hearts will change society."

I found that insistence distressing, since it failed to see the importance of systemic change. I made my point at the time by imagining this scenario. Suppose that Billy Graham preached a message one night that was heard by every person in South Africa—a country deeply immersed at the time in the racist policies and practices of apartheid. And suppose that in response everyone in that country gave their hearts to Christ. The next morning South Africa would be a country full of "saved" individuals—praise the Lord!

The nation, however, would still have a huge racial problem. The overwhelming systemic realities of racial injustice would be unaffected. Laws would need to be changed; the stories about South Africa's past would have to be rewritten; caricatures and jokes would have to be critically examined; new patterns of education and commercial practices would have to be initiated; the physical boundaries separating the races would have to be eradicated.

In the United States some of those necessary structural moves have actually been accomplished over the past decades. No more separate drinking fountains or segregated lunch counters. Major voting rights legislation has been put into effect. Affirmative action programs have been initiated. But more recently we have also been seeing some very visible setbacks: white supremacy rallies, high-level efforts at voter suppression, new patterns of resegregation in our schools, and much more.

I still agree with the arguments I endorsed four decades ago, against "Only changed hearts will change society." What needs to be said these days, though, is that the basic problem with

that line is the word "only." Changed hearts are not enough—
but they are necessary.

Again, the struggle against injustice requires legislation and
the promotion of practices that advance the cause of justice. This
was brought home to me in my late teens—the late 1950s—when
I heard an African American church leader address a denominational gathering. After hearing several people proclaim—in a
debate about a proposal against racial discrimination—that "we
need love and not laws," he told about driving across the country
to attend that meeting. He and his wife had been refused service in restaurants along the way. Referring to one waitress who
simply ignored their request to be seated, he said, "It would be
wonderful if that waitress *loved* us. But right then we were not
asking for love—we wanted *cheeseburgers!*"

I am grateful that these days that couple would be seated at
that restaurant and served their cheeseburgers. But there is still
no guarantee that the waitress would necessarily *love* them, even
given the structural changes that have taken place since she turned
them away. Nor is there reason to be certain that she would likely
be more loving if she belonged to an evangelical church. ·

What would have to happen to that waitress in her church
to nurture a more loving heart toward black persons? We can
certainly hope that she would be taught in church that racism
is a theological heresy, a denial of the created dignity that God
has invested in all human beings by creating them in his own
image. But it is difficult to imagine that such a teaching would be
totally unfamiliar to her, even if it was not put in exactly those
terms. She could well have been taught as a child to sing, "Red
and yellow, black and white, they are precious in his sight, Jesus
loves the little children of the world." And surely she would have
heard sermons about the Good Samaritan and the Golden Rule.

It should not surprise us, though, if these lessons do not take
in the deep places of her soul. Some other things must also be

at work. A genuine Christian love of others requires a working by the Holy Spirit in a person's life.

I hope it is obvious that we evangelicals have some important work to do these days in nurturing that love of others. Ultimately, doctrines of racial superiority can be destroyed only by the deep conviction that each human being is created in the very image of God. But how do we get there? In our present context, we evangelicals can best promote the shared humanness cause by concentrating in a special way on the bond that the Spirit wants us to nurture by exploring our identity in Christ.

The problem of race relations is not simply out there in the patterns and structures of our shared humanity. It is a brutal reality within the Christian community. Nor will answers come simply by clear theological teaching. In my evangelical upbringing I learned early on that all human beings are created in the divine image. The problem is that somehow that teaching did not take in a way that motivated us to engage actively in the struggle for racial justice.

We can implement some important movement toward a sense of our kinship with all humans by beginning within the life of the church itself. Our intra-Christian bond is not just one more thing we might hope to cultivate. It gets at our fundamental identity as believers. The book of Revelation makes this clear: the Lamb who was slain shed his blood to make us into a new kind of kingdom, drawn from "every tribe and people and language and nation" (Rev. 5:9), "a great multitude that no one could count," singing the song of victory to the Lamb (7:9).

This is who we *are*. As individuals we are made into new creatures, but we are also given a new communal identity that comes not from the racial or ethnic blood that flows in our veins but from the blood that was shed on Calvary.

How do we get ourselves beyond a formal acknowledgment of that identity to the realization of the actual bond with persons of other races? One key factor that I have witnessed is the role of personal stories by sisters and brothers in Christ whose lives have been deeply impacted by racial injustice: John Perkins's account of his own abuse by local police officers, efforts by Tom Skinner and Bill Pannell to bring the gospel to the black community, Ruth and Bill Bentley creating the National Association of Black Evangelicals out of a deep concern to promote a commitment to a holistic biblical Christianity, the powerful preaching of James Earl Massey, the witness of those who stayed with us over the years in various parachurch ministries during decades when their important contributions were not always properly acknowledged.

These days we desperately need the stories from flesh-and-blood individuals. White congregations should not just be challenged to love black people. They must be given the opportunity to grieve over the ways Jamaal is treated in the fifth grade, and to pray for strength for Janelle as she struggles to nurture her children's faith as a single mother surrounded by poverty.

We need creative thinking about how to make this happen. In some contexts it can mean bringing families together for meals. In others it may require a creative use of technology: an all-white church in rural Nebraska can show weekly videos of black Christians in Omaha sharing their prayer requests. Other ideas include book clubs discussing novels and biographies, concerts, or film discussions. Our theological conversations certainly need to keep going. But we need more—real experiences within the body of Christ that nurture a desire to promote our mutual growth in the Spirit as we prepare for the culmination of God's purposes in human history.

Speaking prophetically to the larger culture about the heresy of white supremacy is certainly an important thing to do. But it will be effective only if that prophetic word comes from a community that actually embodies the love that alone can strengthen the structures of justice.

| Cultivating Virtues

The late Ronald Thiemann of Harvard Divinity School made good sense when he argued that local congregations should function as "'schools of public virtue,' communities that seek to form the kind of character necessary for public life."[2] It is in the sacred space of our worshiping life that we can draw on the springs of spiritual renewal that can be found only by confessing our sins together in the midst of a people who have responded to the call to worship the living God. And it is in that space that we can experience character formation in the deep places, as we hear the promise that "suffering produces perseverance; [and] perseverance, character; and character, hope. And hope does not put us to shame, because God's love has been poured into our hearts through the Holy Spirit, who has been given to us" (Rom. 5:3–5).

Recent surveys regarding public perceptions of evangelicals— including reports about how younger evangelicals view the older generations—report that evangelicalism has a reputation of encouraging mean-spiritedness and judgmentalism. Much of this, I am convinced, is a sign of the failure to provide effective spiritual formation in the life of the worshiping community. We should want Christians to leave a worship service with a reinforced identity as agents of God's work in the world. One of the most exciting discussions taking place these days about the church is the idea of the missional church. We come to church to encounter the living God. And that God sends us forth from the church back into the world to serve him. The

2. Ronald Thiemann, *Constructing a Public Theology: The Church in a Pluralistic Culture* (Louisville: Westminster John Knox, 1991), 43.

worship service must also be a place where we receive instructions for that sending out.

And the instructions—which ought not to go into practical detail about public policy topics—must be clear about who we are and how we are to find our place in the larger culture during this time of God's patience. Evangelicals, especially those who have been associated with the Religious Right, have often been labeled by our critics as "theocrats." Properly understood, that characterization is not misdirected—as long as it is properly understood. If the earth, with all that is in it, is truly under the sovereign rule of God, then all of reality does indeed constitute a theocracy—a God-ruled domain. In saying this, however, we have to be keenly aware that many of our fellow citizens do not acknowledge the reality of God's rule over all things. We live in a pluralistic democracy wherein our worldview is one among many.

There is coming a day, of course, when "every knee should bow, in heaven and on earth and under the earth, and every tongue acknowledge that Jesus Christ is Lord, to the glory of God the Father" (Phil. 2:10–11). But that day has not yet arrived. Thus we live presently "in the time of God's patience."

Our engagement in the worshiping community of the local congregation is a primary place wherein we cultivate the patience and other virtues that are necessary for our active participation in the larger society. Our worshiping life—singing, praying, the fellowship of the table, the hearing of the Word proclaimed—is a time when we enter, in a special way, into the presence of our King, who then sends us forth to serve the cause of his kingdom in our daily lives. Our efforts at discernment, then, begin in this worshiping context. But again, it is not enough for us, having worshiped together, simply to go off on our own into the world over which he also rules. Diplomats who serve as agents of a specific government also need to engage in policy formation, applying the general goals and values of their government to specific diplomatic missions. Some of this policy formation for us as believers can certainly take place within the context of the institutional church: church education classes, study groups, lectures, and panels. But "church as organism"—parachurch—vocational gatherings, where we address more specific agenda questions, are also important as extended discussions of what we have experienced in the throne room.

And we desperately need those extended discussions. The practical answers to our questions about political specifics do not typically come easily. We certainly cannot arrive at answers simply by looking up specific verses in the Scriptures. On my reading of the relevant biblical passages, for example, I am convinced that the human fetus in the womb is a person, and that this means that I must oppose abortion-on-demand. But how do I follow through on that conviction in the practical realities of political life? Do I work with those who seek to reverse existing pro-abortion legislation? Do I allow for exceptions in cases of rape and incest? Do I—given the realities of life in a democratic pluralism—focus primarily on reducing the number of abortions?

This is only one case in point for the steps that need to be taken in going from what we accept as clear biblical teaching on a given area of concern to the practical questions of political strategy. Those steps must be taken, and they require respectful dialogue within the community of believers, accompanied by much prayer and mutual exploration of wisdom from the Christian past, all under the authority of the written Word that points us to the supreme lordship of Jesus Christ.

| Humility

We evangelicals have often been arrogant in our attitudes toward political life. Sometimes that arrogance has taken the form of a refusal to take seriously the issues of justice and peace. On other occasions we have arrogantly pursued political and legal takeover strategies. We live in times when our efforts to serve the cause of the kingdom will be helped by much self-examination.

John Calvin had it right when he identified humility as basic to Christian spirituality: "I have always been exceedingly delighted," the Reformer wrote, "with the words of Chrysostom, 'The foundation of our philosophy is humility'; and still more with those of Augustine, 'As the orator, when asked, What is the first precept in eloquence? answered, Delivery: What is the second? Delivery: What the third? Delivery: so, if you ask me in regard to the precepts of the Christian Religion, I will answer, first, second, and third, Humility.'"[3]

The persistent habit of careful self-examination requires a spirit of humility, including in our political lives. In an important book that he wrote on civility, John Murray Cuddihy insists that Christians spend time concentrating on the gap between our present imperfection and our future glorification. Doing so, he argues, can help us to formulate an "ethic for the interim" that prescribes patience as we await God's future victory over the forces of unrighteousness.[4]

Cuddihy is right. We do live in an interim period politically. It is presently the time of God's patience with a world still permeated by sin. We also know, though, that God's patience is not that of an uncaring deity who simply allows evil free play until a future divine intervention. Our own participation in the divine patience, then, cannot mean that we tolerate the status quo. We anticipate the final coming of the kingdom in

3. John Calvin, *Institutes of the Christian Religion*, ed. John T. McNeill, trans. Ford Lewis Battles (Philadelphia: Westminster, 1960), II.11.11, pp. 268–69.
4. John Murray Cuddihy, *No Offense: Civil Religion and Protestant Taste* (New York: Seabury Press, 1978), 202.

its fullness by actively working to achieve specific—if only partial—manifestations of that kingdom.

| Kingdom and King

When many of us got going on evangelical social activism in the early 1970s, we placed an emphasis on the importance of kingdom theology. It was a new emphasis for most of us, even though we had all been raised on heavy doses of "King" and "kingdom" imagery: "kingdom causes," "souls added to the kingdom," "walking with the King," "hail him as thy matchless King." Somehow, though, this had not been applied in our evangelical churches to political realities. There was no preaching about the importance of race relations in the kingdom, or about encouraging a critical examination of military policies, or of the issues of economic injustice.

I'm a fan of the writings of James Smith, who has been addressing kingdom themes in creative ways in recent years. The title of his most recent book is especially gratifying to me: *Awaiting the King*.[5] While I was very excited in the 1970s about the ways we were exploring the sociopolitical realities of the kingdom, I did worry a bit about too much kingdom and not enough King. My own efforts sometimes encouraged this imbalance—but I did worry about it frequently. The gospel is more than about a personal relationship with Jesus—but it is not *less* than that. In the next chapter I am going to spend some time explaining why the preservation of the importance of that personal relationship to the King should be seen as a nonnegotiable element in our evangelical legacy.

---

5. James K. A. Smith, *Awaiting the King: Reforming Public Theology* (Grand Rapids: Baker Academic, 2017).

14

"Jesus Died for Me"

Many of us in the evangelical world have devoted much effort toward remedying what we see as an unhealthy individualist focus in our ranks.[1] I can point, for example, to many articles in *Christianity Today* and other evangelical periodicals in the past several decades where evangelicals are called to depart from the notion that all that matters is that individuals get saved and prepare for a heavenly reward. Much evangelical attention has been paid to systemic injustice, social structures, the central importance of "body life," and so on.

In all of this, however, there is an important nuance. We evangelicals never downplay the importance of individuals—as individuals—coming to a saving faith in Jesus Christ. We never say that an individual's very personal relationship to God is not important. What we do say is that individual salvation is *not enough*. In my own thinking on this subject, which has made much of the centrality of the church and the importance

1. The discussion in this section is adapted from Richard J. Mouw, "The Heresy of 'Individualism'?," *Christianity Today*, July 15, 2009, https://www.christianitytoday.com/ct/2009/julyweb-only/128-31.0.html. Used with permission.

of collective Christian address to the issues of injustice and public morality, there are actual stories that have reinforced my convictions about the importance of individual salvation.

Here is one that has stuck with me from my younger years. A man, a prominent leader in his local church, testified that before becoming a Christian he had lived a dissolute life. A salesperson who was constantly on the road, he engaged in considerable immoral activity. One evening, sitting alone in his hotel room, he became very despondent. He did not want another evening spent in the hotel bar. Remembering that there was usually a Gideon Bible in one of the drawers in hotel rooms, he found the Scriptures and began to read the passages recommended in the inside cover under the heading "Feeling Discouraged?" As he read the prescribed passages, he was overcome by a sense of his sin, and finally he fell to his knees and pleaded with God to do something in his life. That experience was the turning point for him. When he told his wife about this, she too wanted a relationship with Christ. They sought out a church, and together they matured in the Christian life.

That story has always fit well with my views of salvation and the church. In a profound sense, of course, the church was a living reality in that hotel room—the invitation extended to him by the placing of a Gideon Bible in that room was as "churchly" a reality as any evangelistic sermon preached from a pulpit. But what the Lord, through the placing of that volume, was doing in the privacy of that hotel room was inviting an individual sinner to bring the burden of his sin and guilt to the cross of Calvary. The man accepted that invitation, and he rightly moved on to the point of identifying himself with the body of Christ.

We evangelicals can tell many stories of that sort. Call that "individualism" if you want. But for us not only is it not heresy, but it is also at the heart of what it means to affirm the gospel of Jesus Christ.

| On Individualism

My own efforts to get at a proper understanding of how the term "individualism" is used rather loosely were stimulated by two conversations I had in the 1970s. One was with a political leader in South Africa's apartheid government. I pressed him about the ways in which his government's segregationist laws denied black citizens many of their basic human rights, and he finally retorted with an irritated tone, "You Americans are so individualistic!" The other was with a European theologian who had said some negative things about the idea of a "personal salvation." When I argued with him on the subject, he shot back, "I don't know how to argue with you evangelicals. You are simply too individualistic!"

In both cases it struck me that maybe being individualistic wasn't such a bad thing. Individual humans are, in the words of the Declaration of Independence, "endowed by their Creator with certain inalienable rights." And the biblical psalms are full of individual declarations: "The LORD is *my* shepherd, *I* shall not want" (Ps. 23:1 NRSV).

To be sure, there clearly are bad ways of emphasizing the importance of the human individual. In their influential book, *Habits of the Heart*, Robert Bellah and his associates told the story of a woman whom they had interviewed named Sheila Larson, who told the interviewers that she follows the dictates of a religion she described as "Sheilaism"—a religion that centered on her own needs and desires. The basic teaching of this religion is, as Sheila put it, "just try to love yourself and be gentle with yourself," and building on that foundation, Sheila also saw a need to love and be gentle with those who were closest to her.[2]

2. Robert Bellah et al., *Habits of the Heart: Individualism and Commitment in American Life* (Los Angeles: University of California Press, 1985), 221. I also discuss this in my chapter "'Magnify, Come Glorify . . .': Some Thoughts about Throne Room Worship," in *The Pastor and the Kingdom: Essays Honoring*

"Sheilaism" came to be used at the time as an expression of the worst sort of American individualism, and understandably so. But in fairness to Sheila, she did see a focus on loving herself as a basis for extending love to others as well. In my own critique of the really bad sort of individualism, I pointed to Frederick Perls's "Gestalt Prayer," which was popular in the "self-actualization" movement at the time.

> I do my thing, and you do yours.
> I am not in this world to live up to your expectations.
> And you are not in this world to live up to mine.
> You are you, and I am I.
> And if by chance we find each other, it's beautiful.
> If not, it can't be helped.[3]

Perls is certainly expressing an extreme form of individualism. It is illuminating, though, to compare Perls's wording with this paragraph from a letter that the former slave Frederick Douglass wrote to the slave owner from whom he had escaped: "I am myself; you are yourself; we are two distinct persons, equal persons. What you are, I am. You are a man, and so am I. God created both, and made us separate beings. I am not by nature bound to you, or you to me. Nature does not make your existence depend upon me, or mine to yours. . . . In leaving you, I took nothing but what belonged to me."[4]

The wording is strikingly similar, with one important exception. Douglass makes it clear that his unique individuality—as

Jack W. Hayford, ed. Jon Huntzinger and S. David Moore (Southlake, TX: Gateway Academic and TKU Press, 2017), 255–67.

3. Frederick S. Perls, *Gestalt Therapy Verbatim*, ed. John O. Stevens (New York: Bantam Books, 1969), 4. The critique I mention is in the chapter on individualism in my book *The God Who Commands: A Study in Divine Command Ethics* (Notre Dame: University of Notre Dame Press, 1991).

4. Frederick Douglass, *My Bondage and My Freedom* (New York: Arno, 1968), 423.

well as that of his former owner—is grounded in the will of God. Each person is a divine creation, which means that each is ultimately responsible to God alone. No human creature has the right to claim to "own" another.

In his marvelous study of black slave spirituality, the theologian James Cone refers to the "existential 'I'" that gets expressed in the slave spirituals. "Nobody knows the trouble *I've* seen / Nobody knows but Jesus." "When *I* get to heaven *I'm* going to put on my shoes / and walk all over God's heaven." In the midst of the oppressiveness of the slavery system, Cone observes, the Christian slave "knew that he alone was accountable to God, because somewhere in the depth of the soul's search for meaning, he met the divine."[5]

Cone rightly insists that we should not see this "I"-centered slave spirituality as just one more expression of nineteenth-century revivalism. It was born out of a deep struggle against wicked racist denials of the humanity of African Americans. But the case that he makes does demonstrate the need to look beyond the mere language of "I-ness" to the broader dynamics of selfhood. Douglass proclaimed "I am myself" as a rejection of the racist insistence that he was a mere commodity to be bought and sold. The salesman reading the Gideon Bible can affirm his unique selfhood as an acknowledgment of a guilt and shame for which he is fully responsible.

| "For Me"

At the heart of a proper evangelical affirmation of the existential "I" is the recognition of the reality that each individual self lives his or her life, to use a Latin phrase much loved in the

5. James H. Cone, *The Spirituals and the Blues: An Interpretation* (New York: Seabury, 1972), 67–68.

Christian tradition, *coram deo*—roughly, "before the face of God." Psalm 139 is very much a *coram deo* prayer.

> You have searched me, LORD,
>   and you know me.
> You know when I sit and when I rise;
>   you perceive my thoughts from afar.
> You discern my going out and my lying down;
>   you are familiar with all my ways.
>
> Psalm 139:1–3

To be known in this profoundly intimate manner—to be known by someone who knows us much better than we know ourselves—is in many ways a frightening thing. God actually knows all of our thoughts and fantasies, our hopes and fears. Frightening, indeed. But it also serves to inspire our sense of wonder about the gift of salvation, as expressed in these hymn lyrics from Charles Wesley, "Died he *for me,* who caused his pain?" or these from John Newton, "Amazing grace . . . that saved a wretch *like me.*"

| A Complex Cross

In chapter 9 I referred to the sense of mystery that has characterized much evangelical spirituality, and I complained that this does not automatically translate into an acknowledgment of mystery in our theological formulations. This disconnect seems clear to me in our theology of Christ's atoning work, particularly with reference to the "he died for me" element in traditional evangelicalism. One way to group the different strands of atonement theology is under two headings: vertical and horizontal. The vertical category depicts, in different ways, the central significance of the cross in terms of a transaction that took place within the Trinity, typically between the Father and the Son: Jesus offered himself up to the Father; he paid a debt that we humans could not pay on our own; he hung in our place, offering himself as a sacrifice for sin.

The horizontal conceptions see what happened on the cross as primarily a transaction between Jesus and humankind. He showed us the nature of true forgiveness by refusing to be vindictive toward those who were putting him to death; he modeled for us the nature of self-sacrificial love; in the midst of his own extreme suffering he expressed a concern for the well-being of others.

The influential modernist preacher Harry Emerson Fosdick was a thoroughgoing horizontal who described the vertical position in this way in his classic 1922 sermon "Shall the Fundamentalists Win?": the defenders of the traditionalist view of redemption, he says, insist "that we must believe in a special theory of the Atonement—that the blood of our Lord, shed in a substitutionary death, placates an alienated Deity and makes possible welcome for the returning sinner."[6] That kind of negative depiction has taken on an even harsher tone in recent years, as some feminist theologians have characterized the vertical views as portrayals of "divine child abuse." The most extreme version of this characterization has come from Joanne Carlson Brown, who argues that Christianity has to purge itself of the idea of a "bloodthirsty God," one who requires that "a blood sin upon the whole human race can be washed away only by the blood of the lamb." All of this must be rejected, she says: "We do not need to be saved by Jesus' death from some original sin. We need to be liberated from this abusive patriarchy."[7]

6. Harry Emerson Fosdick, "Shall the Fundamentalists Win?," *Christian Work* 102 (June 10, 1922): 716–22; available online at http://historymatters.gmu.edu/d/5070.
7. Joanne Carlson Brown, "Divine Child Abuse," *Daughters of Sarah* 18, no. 3 (1992): 28.

While not addressing the "child abuse" objection explicitly, the great John Stott has offered a helpful way of responding to this kind of criticism when he warns evangelicals against adopting any picture of the atonement in which the Son is a victim who stands *over against* a Father who is in turn "a pitiless ogre whose wrath has to be assuaged." Says Stott: "Both God and Christ were subjects not objects, taking the initiative together to save sinners. Whatever happened on the cross in terms of 'God-forsakenness' was voluntarily accepted by both in the same holy love which made atonement necessary." While the words "satisfaction" and "substitution" must never "in any circumstances be given up," Stott argues, we must also be very clear that "the biblical gospel of atonement is of God satisfying himself by substituting himself for us."[8]

The substitutionary theme is still quite alive in evangelical hymnody and theology. But when evangelical social activism emerged in the 1970s, there also was an embrace of a particular horizontal perspective, the *Christus Victor* portrayal of the atonement as made popular by John Howard Yoder in his influential—among activist evangelicals—book *The Politics of Jesus*. Here Yoder places a strong emphasis on Calvary as a decisive encounter with the powers of evil. The human authorities, representing political, economic, military, and religious forces of the day who collectively crucified Jesus, were in fact acting in the service of spiritual "principalities and powers," who did all they could to destroy the Son of God. But Jesus "accepted powerlessness, and in doing so had victory over them. His death and resurrection are clear testimony to the futility of relying on violence and other forms of coercive

8. John R. W. Stott, *The Cross of Christ* (Downers Grove, IL: InterVarsity, 1986), 150–51, 159–60.

power to solve the fundamental problems that plague us in our humanness."[9]

When I introduced the horizontal category above, I characterized it as representing those views that see the cross as a kind of ethical teaching event. In his dying Jesus *shows us* something about how we are to live. The *Christus Victor* view goes a step beyond that. It is not vertical in that it explains what happened on the cross without making explicit reference to some transaction that took place, as it were, within the Trinity. Rather, it sees the death of Christ as a dramatic encounter with the spiritual principalities and powers—which shows us how we are to live our lives in response to that encounter. We too must confront the evil powers, refusing to be held captive to the various "isms" that they use to hold us in their sway—militarism, consumerism, and the like. While we outwardly live within the social structures over which they claim to have authority, we do so in the confidence that they are already defeated enemies. Thus we follow the example of Christ, who allowed the visible authorities to nail him to the cross—a "voluntary subordination of one who knows that another regime is normative."[10] The fate of the evil powers has been sealed. To use their coercive methods to try to defeat them is to fail to grasp the victory that has been achieved by accepting the "powerlessness" of the cross.

This view, of course, has significant advantages over the more liberal "be like Jesus" approach of Fosdick. The most obvious difference is that the *Christus Victor* perspective insists on a strongly supernatural account of the redemptive mission of Jesus. The crucified Christ does not merely provide us with an example of how to live; he also makes that life possible by a decisive engagement with the spiritual forces of evil. He did

---

9. John Howard Yoder, *The Politics of Jesus* (Grand Rapids: Eerdmans, 1972), 146.
10. Yoder, *Politics*, 137.

something on our behalf that is of cosmic importance: he *defeated* the principalities and powers. His resurrection is a clear proclamation of his victory.

While I have serious disagreements with some of the ethical aspects of Yoder's approach, I have learned much from his perspective. Christ's redemptive work certainly does have real implications for our lives as consumers and citizens. The multifaceted work of the cross did indeed include a decisive encounter with the invisible powers of evil. The biblical basis for the *Christus Victor* depiction is set forth clearly and succinctly in Colossians 2:15, where the apostle Paul says that Jesus "disarmed the powers and authorities, [making] a public spectacle of them, triumphing over them by the cross."

What I find missing in many presentations of the *Christus Victor* perspective, though, is the biblical insistence on a clear link between this aspect of Christ's atoning work and the "he died for me" aspect of the other biblical themes. Indeed, that link is clearly on display in the passage I just cited from Colossians 2. The reference there to the "disarming" of the evil powers is immediately preceded by this characterization of the substitutionary work of the cross: "When you were dead in your sins and in the uncircumcision of your flesh, God made you alive with Christ. He forgave us all our sins, having canceled the charge of our legal indebtedness, which stood against us and condemned us; he has taken it away, nailing it to the cross" (Col. 2:13–14).

That the two perspectives—"substitution" (vertical) and "disarming the powers" (horizontal)—must be held together within a biblically faithful understanding of the atoning work of Christ is well understood by N. T. Wright. He has been a strong defender in recent years of the *Christus Victor* perspective—so much so that some of his evangelical critics have charged him with simply denying the substitutionary dimension of the atonement. But not so. Here is Wright: "Jesus, the innocent one, was drawing on to himself the holy wrath of God against human sin in general, so that human sinners like you and me can find, as we look at the cross, that the load of sin and guilt we have been carrying is taken away from us."[11]

Each of our individual burdens of shame and guilt have been nailed to the cross.[12] Evangelicals have always insisted on that message as central to the proclamation of the gospel. Again, there are a variety of images for capturing this emphasis. What they have in common is this: they point us to the fact that on the cross of Calvary, Jesus did something for us that we could never do for ourselves as sinners. He engaged in a transaction that has eternal consequences for our standing before a righteous God.

| A "Second Naivete" Testimony

I can't explain why I have done so much with this subject here without also adding a personal testimony.

On a Monday evening in September 1975, while on my post-doctoral fellowship at Princeton University, I went to my first Alcoholics Anonymous (AA) meeting. I had two scholarly goals that year: one was to explore some issues in social theory and the other was to finish writing a book dealing with Christianity and politics. For the latter project, questions about atonement theory loomed large for me.

But I had also come to Princeton with a very personal goal that I had talked about with no one else. I wanted to get control

11. N. T. Wright, *The Crown and the Fire: Meditations on the Cross and the Life of the Spirit* (Grand Rapids: Eerdmans, 1992), 51.
12. I first made this observation about shame and guilt being nailed to the cross in my article "Getting to the Crux of Calvary," *Christianity Today*, June 4, 2012, https://www.christianitytoday.com/ct/2012/may/getting-to-the-crux-of-cal vary.html?ctlredirect=true.

over my use of alcohol. My drinking had gotten to a crisis point: a couple of my Calvin College colleagues had expressed their worries about me; I was lying to others about my patterns of consumption; I had experienced some scary blackouts.

I blamed it all on the stress of full-time teaching and other academic responsibilities. Our year at Princeton was to be a time to bring things under control. Instead, for the first couple of weeks in New Jersey it only got worse. I became desperate. I was convinced I was simply going to drink myself to death. On a Sunday evening I finally uttered the words out loud to my wife, Phyllis, while sobbing uncontrollably: "I'm an alcoholic, and I don't know what to do." We agreed I would turn to AA.

As I walked the six blocks on Monday evening to my first AA meeting, I sang the same words that I did when nineteen years earlier I walked the aisles of Madison Square Garden in response to Billy Graham's invitation: "Just as I am without one plea, but that thy blood was shed for me." This time, though, I was screaming those words in my soul, in utter desperation. Jesus was waiting for me at AA, and as I write this I have had over four decades of sobriety.

N. T. Wright insists that in addition to Christ's victory over the principalities and powers, he also took what is for each of us our "load of sin and guilt" onto himself on the cross of Calvary. The night I walked in desperation to my first AA meeting, I was in the midst of writing about theories of the atonement. The power of the gospel to confront the systemic "isms" that plague us in our collective lives was high on my intellectual agenda. But that evening was a "second naivete" experience for me (see chapter 4). In those moments nothing was more important to me than the existential awareness that Jesus shed his blood on Calvary "for me."

More recently I overheard a conversation between a couple of young evangelical pastors at a coffee break during a conference. One of them was saying rather forcefully that he seldom mentions the substitutionary work of Christ anymore in his sermons. Instead, he said, he talks about how Christ encountered "the powers of consumerism, militarism, racism, and super-patriotism." I was conflicted about what I heard. The concern for the systemic aspects of the Christian message was laudable. But those concerns will not take proper root in evangelical hearts unless those hearts have known what it is like to hear the call to discipleship from the Savior—the Innocent One—who has carried their "load of sin and guilt" to the cross of Calvary.

I don't want evangelicals to lose that key element in our legacy. We need the "second naivete" on this. And for those who are moving into the "formerly known as" category, if some of us who presently are sticking with the label have to make the move also sometime in the future, it will be important that we can bring this with us—to be welcomed by "formerly known as" friends who still love the Savior who went to the cross for them.

But on that subject of staying or going, I still have some brief thoughts to share.

| 15 |

Holding On
While Staying Restless

The philosopher Alasdair MacIntyre has said that a healthy tradition is one where people in that tradition keep debating about what is essential to the vitality of the tradition.[1] The debate over the continuing usefulness of the "evangelical" label can be a healthy one if we pursue it together with a clear sense of the realities that we must take into account.

One reality is that American evangelicalism is a movement encompassing a complex network of organizations and parachurch ministries. I once talked to a consultant on evangelical charitable giving who offered this profile of the kind of donors that I should be connecting with as Fuller Seminary's president: This kind of couple supports their local church, which is a high priority for them. They also give to a Christian college or campus ministry. They are enthusiastic about Young Life and World Vision. Furthermore, they subscribe to *Christianity Today* and

1. Alasdair MacIntyre, *After Virtue: A Study in Moral Theory*, 2nd ed. (Notre Dame, IN: University of Notre Dame Press, 1984), 221.

have some favorite authors, such as John Ortberg and Anne Lamott. Nor is that, for them, a set of disconnected causes. There is a pattern in their minds, one which they may not be able to explain with precision—but it is generally captured for them by "evangelical."

The kind of network he was describing is still fairly influential in the present evangelical world. And none of the organizations or individuals mentioned could be seen as tied into the highly politicized evangelicalism that is getting so much attention these days. So here is a question I think is worth asking: When we resign from evangelicalism, are we disassociating ourselves from, say, *Christianity Today* and Young Life and World Vision? If so, why? Can't we at least identify with what they embody as evangelicals? We owe it at least to explain ourselves to this network. Evangelical writer Ann Voskamp has many devoted readers, with several of her books appearing on the *New York Times* best-seller list. What do we have to say to them when we decide that we no longer want to be known as evangelicals?

Another reality is the global context. This factor looms very large for me. The World Evangelical Alliance reports that it serves churches and organizations around the world, representing six hundred million evangelicals. One recent poll suggests that about 24 percent of the US population self-identify as evangelicals—nearly 78 million people.[2] Perhaps there is inflation of numbers here, but let's take them as given. This says that there are half a billion evangelicals living beyond the borders of the United States, the majority of whom are in the Southern Hemisphere.

What do we owe them? In abandoning the "evangelical" label are we setting ourselves apart from them? What do we

2. Bob Smietana, "Many Who Call Themselves Evangelical Don't Actually Hold Evangelical Beliefs," *LifeWay Research*, Dec. 6, 2017, https://lifewayresearch.com/2017/12/06/many-evangelicals-dont-hold-evangelical-beliefs/.

have to say now, especially to those leaders in Africa, Asia, and Latin America who have studied in our institutions and have returned to their own countries with a profound commitment to the gospel?

In *Freedom of the Will*, Jonathan Edwards explains why he continues to call himself a Calvinist in this way: "However the term 'Calvinist' is in these days, amongst most, a term of greater reproach than the term 'Arminian'; yet I should not take it at all amiss, to be called a Calvinist, for distinction's sake."[3]

That "for distinction's sake" test is a significant one for me. I have long called myself an evangelical because I haven't wanted to be identified with theological liberalism. But we can certainly arrive at a point where a label is no longer helpful "for distinction's sake." Like many of my friends these days, I don't want to be called an evangelical if that gives the impression I am a mean-spirited right-winger. If that is what the label has come to, then I am willing to give it up. The cause of the gospel is too important to be impeded by nostalgia or stubbornness.

But I do need to say it bluntly: simply to announce that I—my existential "I"—no longer wants to be known as an evangelical strikes me as an expression of an unhealthy individualism. For one thing, it allows me to define evangelical realities in a very American way, ignoring the way half a billion people in other parts of the world experience being evangelical.

An African evangelical leader who had been trained in our evangelical institutions recently returned to the United States for a visit. "What is going on in American evangelicalism?" he asked me. "We hear some pretty strange things. You are the folks who taught us to be firm in our faith, and now you seem to be drifting in weird directions. We are praying for you,

---

3. Jonathan Edwards, *The Freedom of the Will, Works of Jonathan Edwards*, ed. Paul Ramsey (New Haven: Yale University Press, 1957), 131.

that there will be a revival here of what you taught us to take back home!" Folks like him need to be important conversation partners about what evangelical identity means today. We not only owe them that engagement, but we also need to welcome them—those who were once our students—to be our teachers now.

For me, the only way to be a properly functioning evangelical is to keep arguing about what it means to *be* an evangelical. Restlessness in claiming that label has long been the way I have kept moving. I hope that many of us can stay restless as we hold on while exploring together whether the best way to remain faithful to the legacy is to let go of the label.

When past evangelicals became disillusioned with a specific movement or association, they typically adopted one of two strategies: either they "split" as a group, moving on to form a new collective entity that claimed to be the true continuation of the legacy of that from which they had separated, or they stayed on, praying and working for a revival within the present association.

The former option often put on clear display the worst sort of evangelical separatism. But it did at least have this virtue: it was a *communal* strategy. The other option had its drawbacks, but it could draw on inspiration from past renewal movements.

My own assessment is that each of those strategies is preferable to simply drifting off one by one in diverse directions. For the present, I am inclined to go with the second option—working for evangelical renewal, rather than simply allowing the movement's label to be co-opted by leaders who have departed from the best of the legacy. And one of the advantages of the "revival" effort is that we have folks in Africa—and likely elsewhere—praying that we will succeed.

Index